THE TRIPLE SOLDIER
And my Mother

A True Story

ANDREW FARON

Published in 2017 by Andrew Faron

This book is copyright. Except for private study, research, criticism or reviews, as permitted under the Copyright Act, no part of this book may be reproduced, stored in a retrieval system or transmitted in any form or by any means without prior written permission from the publisher.

Copyright © Andrew Faron 2017

Cataloguing-in-Publication details available from
the National Library of Australia

ISBN: 978-0-6480101-0-4 (pbk)

Also available as an ebook
ISBN: 978-0-6480101-1-1 (ebk)

Cover and book layout design
by Publicious Book Publishing
www.publicious.com.au

Cover image: Vintage Landscape Fabric Background © Diana Rich (Fotolia)

DISCLAIMER
With respect to my parents their real names are used, as well as mine. All other names of characters in this publication have been changed to protect those still living. Any resemblance to real people, living or dead is purely coincidental. I have no letters before or behind my name and claim no literary scholarship. I have written this book from my heart in gratitude to my parents, who retold their experiences to me, as to what happened to them during WWII.

DEDICATION

This book is dedicated to my Niece, Monique *(nee Faron)*
who wanted to know her heritage

IN MEMORY OF MY PARENTS

Franciczek Faron 1913 – 1978
Maria Malgorzata Faron 1920 – 2005

They gave me life, love and the opportunity to write about their war experiences.

It is because of our ancestors that we are here today.

THE TRIPLE SOLDIER And My Mother

INTRODUCTION

The Truth is usually uncomfortable, difficult, unpleasant and inconvenient to deal with; but it should never be deliberately avoided and forgotten. Unfortunately 'Lies' are much more acceptable because they gloss over the reality of life's brutality, prejudice, harshness and the unacceptable truth. The reality of what actually took place during World War Two for my parents was unimaginable but true. It needs to be pointed out, that there are literally millions of war stories with millions of different experiences. However, most people want to forget and move forward. That is how we are made to cope with tragedy and it is a "good" human trait that we are able to move on and laugh again. One must move on or we would all go crazy, but it is also from the past that we need to learn and not just brush it away, as if it never happened.

My father was a self-controlled man of great courage, integrity, respect, humour and responsibility with a very positive outlook on daily life. He always had room for humour in life, no matter how harsh the situation confronted him. He gave me that gift of responsibility, respect and humour, for which I am grateful. He was living with the memory of poverty in his youth and the scars of war throughout his life, but buried them inside him as much as he could. Only on occasion would he speak about some of his experiences, which though intensely painful, I wish today he had told me a lot more. Now that he has gone I do not have enough detailed information of his experiences during World War II. Much of it is lost in time, like the wind blowing into space and so much truth is lost with that generation. He had a very strong Polish accent when he spoke in English and was such an intelligent, honourable and dutiful man, whom I will always admire deeply, love and cherish in my heart. His wisdom and strength of fortitude will always be remembered. He was a wonderful and loving father and a true gentleman.

My mother, on the other hand, was a very different person and a fighter all her life. She was also a woman of integrity, prim and proper as well as a very loving mother, but possessive of her children at times. The scars of war were much more intense for her, because she talked about her experiences more openly to me. Although she was a very patient and strong minded woman, it was perhaps a way for her to deal with the dark ghosts of the past and move on, day by day, when the memories were too arduous to bear. She spoke English very well with a charming Polish accent that everyone loved. She was a wonderful cook, a professional milliner and an amazingly talented dress maker. She liked the finer things in life and paid attention to respect, good manners and behaviour, which she taught to her children. When she went out she always dressed elegantly. She was a tenacious person, vibrant, strong, resolute and emotionally very much more expressive than my father. Yet she also had a wonderful sense of humour with laugher, joie de vivre and fun.

"I loved them dearly and miss them deeply."

Joy and sorrow go hand in hand, thus allowing us to experience and know the difference. Only then we can compare and know what it is like to be happy or sad. With such understanding we gain a sense of compassion, empathy and love for another human being. Life is filled with both happiness and tragedy no matter how rich or poor one may be.

Before you proceed to read the whole story I wish to mention that millions of people, of my generation, have also been deeply affected by World War Two (WWII), who had parents living in Europe at the time or in the battle zones of the world. Thousands of people became known as DPs; "Displaced Persons or Refugees." **I was one of them.**

There were many camps set up for such DPs, which was a

temporary facility for displaced persons. The term is mainly used for camps established after WWII in Germany, Austria, and Italy, primarily for refugees from Eastern Europe and the former inmates of the Nazi German concentration camps. Two years after WWII ended in Europe, some 850,000 people lived in DP camps across Europe, among them Armenians, Poles, Latvians, Lithuanians, Yugoslavs, Jews, Greeks, Russians, Ukrainians and Czechoslovaks.

In reality, after the war ended there were such huge numbers of people world-wide, who were uprooted from their homelands that amounted to a staggering number of DPs. It was estimated between 11 to 20 million people who were displaced.

Since the end of WWII, leading up to and following the Korean and Vietnam Wars, there has never been a stop to the flow of refugees from all parts of the world, fleeing their homelands in the pursuit of finding a safer and better country to live in. It would amount to many millions and we are still counting these displaced people daily. Currently in 2015, violence has forced 60 million people from their homes globally, according to the United Nations High Commission for DPs or Refugees; the highest number since World War II.

After listening to the war experiences from my parents it did affect me throughout my life. I can truthfully say that my brother and I are victims and survivors of the tragedy of WWII by default.

Needless to say the outcome equipped me to try and write their story. There will be a great number of people of Polish descent, as well as other DPs from other countries, who will relate to this story in some parts. They would have had similar experiences, when listening to their parents' stories of what happened to them in war zones.

NB: Please be aware of the reference to the German army, which is also known as the 'Wehrmacht' in German and does appear in the book. The meaning of The Wehrmacht:

> *The Wehrmacht (German pronunciation: Vermaht) "Defence Force" was the unified armed forces of Nazi Germany from 1935 to 1946. It consisted of the Heer* **(army)**, *the Kriegsmarine* **(navy)** *and the Luftwaffe* **(air force)**.

PREFACE

My parents were Polish (Silesian), born in the region of Silesia. The following story is written from my heart, as a testimony to my parents. The truth is painful and brutal at times, but there is also a cleansing of the soul in accepting reality no matter how much it hurts. Only then we can heal and forgive to enable us to move on.

As I begin to write about the brief history of my family during WWII I have to go back in time to Silesia, Germany and the former Czechoslovakia, which is now part of Poland. Although the genealogy of my ancestors goes back to 1814, as far as I know.

It is important to have a brief understanding of what Silesia was and is today. It is part of the border lands of Germany and the present day Czech Republic and Slovakia. I will begin with the turn of the century in the early 1900s, when my parents were born.

The Province of Silesia was a province of the Kingdom of Prussia, existing from 1815 to 1919, when it was divided into the Upper and Lower Silesian provinces, and briefly again from 1938 to 1941. As a Prussian province, Silesia became part of the German Empire during the Prussian-led unification of Germany in 1871.

Silesia is rich in mineral and natural resources and includes several important industrial areas. Silesia's largest city and historical capital is **Wrocław** (German: Breslau). Other large cities are Opole (Oppeln), Gliwice (Gleiwitz), and Katowice (Katowitz) in Poland; Ostrava and Opava in the Czech Republic; and Görlitz (Polish: Zgorzelec) in Germany. Its main river is the Oder (Odra).

Silesia is in the south western area of Poland with Wroclaw as its capital city in the map, which is historically most interesting. However, it is little known about today since Poland has incorporated Silesia after World War II.

Silesia's borders and national affiliation have changed radically over time, both when it was a hereditary possession of noble houses and after the rise of modern nation-states. The first known states to hold power there were those of Greater Moravia at the end of the 9th century and Bohemia early in the 10th century. In the 10th century Silesia was incorporated into the early Polish state, but it later broke into independent duchies, coming under increasing Czech and German influence. It came under the rule of the Crown of Bohemia, which passed to the Austrian Habsburg Monarchy in 1526.

Most of Silesia was conquered by Prussia in 1742, later becoming part of the German Empire, the Weimar Republic and Nazi Germany up to 1945. After WWI the easternmost part of this region was awarded to Poland by the victorious Allies, after rebellions by Silesian Polish people and a plebiscite. After World War II the bulk of Silesia was transferred to a Polish jurisdiction and became part of Poland.

The remaining parts of Silesia which went to Czechoslovakia after the First World War remain so, and are part of the Czech Republic with the part west of the Oder-Neisse line in Germany.

Most inhabitants of Silesia today speak the national languages of their respective countries (Polish, Czech, and German). There is an on-going debate whether a local Silesian speech should be considered a Polish dialect or a separate language. There also exists a Silesian German or Lower Silesian language, although this form of German is almost extinct.

I will relate the story from a collection of my memories, as well as from the many notes I took of what my parents told me. I am grateful to my parents for having shared so many experiences of their lives during World War II, as well as meeting all their Polish friends, while I was growing up in London. Most of all I am immensely thankful to them for teaching me to speak the Polish language, which is a beautiful language, and an asset to treasure and possess. I consider myself very lucky to be able to use it to this day.

It has allowed me to communicate with my family members in Poland and Germany, whom I visit regularly in their homeland respectively. I discovered that knowing another language is like having another soul, because it allows one to enter the mentality of the people in that country. Their culture, emotions, behaviour and humour is so much more understood.

I immigrated to Australia in 1967 from England and joined Qantas Airways in 1971 as cabin crew, making it my career, and stayed with Qantas Airways for 31 years. My exposure to so many different countries, races, languages, religions, cultures, foods, behaviours and social structures, gave me a wonderful and rich insight into the world we live in.

The pursuit of knowledge has always been paramount for me to know and understand life in the world we live in today. I am so grateful to Qantas for giving me the opportunity to travel so extensively through my job and gain such an enriching experience. My endless travels throughout the world since 1960 gave me the greatest education I ever expected.

While growing up at home the only language I spoke with my parents was Polish. All the stories I was told by my parents were in Polish, and as I wrote the following chapters I remember them in the Polish language.

It has a special and sentimental emotional aspect for me, as the language is an emotional one and when I wrote, translating from Polish to English in my mind, I remember the pain in my parents' hearts, eyes and faces, as they related their painful war memories to me. Strangely enough, using English seems to have a less painful aspect than using the Polish language. One's concept of emotion through language becomes more observable as you grow older and walk through the passage of time.

After listening to the unspeakable atrocities of the war experiences from my parents, I have never understood why we have wars in the first place and I still feel the same about it today. It has been a very sentimental journey and a privilege for me to write the following story for my parents. Let us hope that wars will not be repeated 'ad nauseam' in the future.

AUSTRALIA 2014

I woke up at dawn, staggered out of bed and looked at the sky through the window, which had a hint of the rising sun. In the dull light I could still see the moon and a few stars. I heard the first bird sounds already in the trees, announcing the beginning of another day, my heart fluttered with a smile. It was a very special day for me, one that I had been waiting for many months. I made myself a cup of coffee and sat in the quiet of my lounge room, deeply thinking of my niece and family and all that happened since I was with her in 2012. Soon it was time for me to get ready and drive to the hotel on the Gold Coast.

In the very early hours of that day I made my way to meet my niece, Monique and her husband, Mark and two children, Brian and Mandy. As I drove along the empty road, adorned with tall palm trees either side, gently swaying in the ocean breeze, I felt awed by the warm blinding sun and cloudless blue sky. I arrived with apprehension in my stomach and patiently sat waiting in the lobby of the Sheraton Mirage Hotel. I was staring at the ocean feeling a kind of numbness and trepidation with scattered thoughts. I kept looking at my watch, waiting for the arrival of my niece and family from America. Two years had passed since I saw Monique in Los Angeles and much had transpired during that time.

A black limousine arrived outside the hotel lobby. I got up and looked in anticipation if it was my family arriving. Yes it was; I saw the blond hair of Monique, who was the first person to emerge from the car, waving from a distance, followed by the rest of her family. I ran over to greet her and threw my arms around her. Monique was over-joyed to see me again, and I was thrilled to be with her once more. It felt wonderful to be in her loving arms again. After our warm and loving greetings we all went to their room and sat in the lounge of their plush hotel suite. With a big smile Monique looked at me and reached deeply into her suitcase to pull out something, which she handed to me. It was a large package, wrapped in bubble wrap, looking like a picture in a black frame, and with a warm smile on her face she said. "Uncle Andrew, here is what's rightfully yours, open it. I love you."

I sat there staring wide-eyed in anticipation, wondering what it might be, and began to un-wrap the parcel to see what she gave me. It was a framed picture and as I saw what was in the picture I was moved to tears and speechless with what it was. I looked into her eyes and with a sigh I just said;

"Oh Monique! Thank you, thank you so very much from the depth of my heart for all your love and kindness. I don't know what to say."

It opened an emotional journey in my heart, which I shared with my parents, when I wrote the story of my parents' unforgettable experiences during WWII in the pages you are about to read.

CHAPTER ONE

My Father 1913

Under the Polish Flag:

Franciszek Faron was born on 27th September 1913 in Orzesze in the prefecture of Pszczyna in Upper Silesia, now Poland, just before WWI. Only ten months later WW1 broke out in July 1914. His father, my grandfather Andrzej Faron:- 28/08/1872 to 17/07/1927 did participate in that war as a home guard. He was a rich property dealer and unfortunately lost his money through selling off property during an unstable currency crisis in Poland in about 1916. From that time poverty took over the family and my father grew up in hardship. I know very little about my grandparents' history, as all the records are lost in WWI and WWII. Regrettably I never met my paternal grandparents.

One of eight siblings, my father's early education was at a German school, as that part of Upper Silesia was still under the Weimar Republic, which was later re-incorporated back into Poland. He was a great scholar with a rich education at school. He was also a lover of languages and very gifted in learning new languages quickly. My father became well versed in Polish, Silesian dialect, German, Czech and later in life he had a good command of Russian, Ukrainian, French and Italian.

In his youth he won a scholarship at Grammar School *(Gymnasium - in Polish)* and was going to study dentistry at The Jagiellonian University of Krakow, which dates from 1364 and was the oldest centre of learning for many surrounding countries in Europe.

At 23 years of age my father fell in love with a pretty young girl named Maria. In that era mutual respect between a man and woman was very strict and important. My parents met in 1936 on one Sunday morning at mass in church. Maria did not want to sit with her father and stepmother and was sitting alone in the same pew, as did my father, with a few people between them. Maria was a young shy 16 year old girl. They noticed each other and my father was enchanted with her and smiled. Maria smiled back and blushed. He wondered how to meet her so he came up with an idea. After mass was finished he quickly walked out, a few paces ahead of her, and drop his handkerchief in front of her, anticipating that she would hopefully pick it up.

Maria picked up his handkerchief, knowing in her heart that he deliberately did so and said.

"Excuse me mister. You dropped your handkerchief."

As she handed him the handkerchief, with a coquettish smile, he smiled back taking her hand and kissed the back of her hand and introduced himself.

"Thank you. I'm Franus. I'm delighted to meet you. May I have the pleasure of escorting you home?"

Maria was blushing noticeably and felt a bit weak in the knees looking at this handsome blue eyed man with her deep brown eyes. She accepted his proposal to be escorted home. They were both radiant and captured in the moment of meeting. She was also enchanted as was my father. That was how they met and fell in love at first sight. They had a very long courtship and engagement.

Politeness and refined good manners was at its height in that era and well understood in the higher classes of society with such a strict culture. Holding hands during a walk in the park was permissible but passionate kissing was unthinkable, being in such a staunch Catholic country. They were both so in love and deeply respectful to each other, that it appears almost ridiculous and laughable in the 21st century.

By the age of 18 years Maria could no longer endure the cruelty of her stepmother and moved out to a bed-sit flat in Podlesie in late-1938. She was strong willed enough to make such a daring move. In that period a woman normally stayed at home until she married, as it was frowned upon for a single woman living alone. This upheaval in her home created a damaging estrangement between father and daughter, as her father was very strict and totally disapproved of such scandalous behaviour.

My father was conscripted in 1934, as it was compulsory in Poland to serve in the army for two years. Being an Officer of 2nd Lieutenant in the Polish Army, my father was ordered to take part in the war. He was called up from the Polish Army Reserve on 30th August 1939. He took part in the September campaign during the invasion of Poland by Nazi Germany on 1st September 1939. Poland was invaded by Nazi Germany from the West, as well as by Russia from the East sixteen days later. My father's aspiration of becoming a dentist was postponed indefinitely.

Suddenly the parting sorrows began between the Polish soldiers and their loved ones and family on the platforms of the train stations throughout Poland. Soon my father was holding his beloved fiancée Maria in his arms at the train station in Mikolow.

Franciszek, Franus in short, expressed his painful heartfelt parting detachment from the love of his life. He was on tenterhooks and stressed about his departure. He looked at Maria's face with a painful heavy heart having to leave her behind. He so earnestly wanted to show her how much he loved her and this would be the last and only chance left for him to express it, before leaving for the warfront. Never having kissed her passionately before, he knew that it would have to be now or never. Looking at her he said.

"Maria, let me take a long look at your beautiful face, so that I can carry you in my heart with me wherever I go. I love you, remember that."

They embraced and held on to each other in desperation, knowing that it could be for the last time. The moment was disappearing quickly and the whistle blew for the train to depart. Franus squeezed Maria into himself and desperately passionately kissed her lips. He felt so relieved and wonderful to be able to do that and prove his love for her.

Maria's heart was melting with her surrendering lips to Franus with such a confirmation of their impenetrable love for each other, now sealed with one fateful blissful kiss. She stood on the platform embracing him tightly, trembling in gut churning tears of sadness; he let go of her reluctantly and jumped onto the train as it slowly pulled away.

My father was flustered and sat with the rest of the Polish soldiers on the train, looking through the window waving to Maria, but felt so alone suddenly wrenched from Maria's arms. Once she was out of sight he kept seeing her face in his mind, hanging on to that image of Maria and gained the strength to face the unthinkable, when confronting the invading German forces at the Polish German border. He was experiencing a void of life and despondency in his heart with gut wrenching discomfort as to what to expect at the border.

Waving goodbye, with many others running along the platform with the train, Maria yelled out with a bursting heart.

"Franus, go with god's care, I love you. I will be with you."

Standing alone at the end of the platform, wondering if she would ever see him again would have been a dreadful and empty feeling. As the advancing autumn wind gently caressed her hair she lost sight of him and the train, her soul was already feeling lonesome, lost without him. Maria stood still at the end of the platform staring at an empty train track, wondering what will happen to him.

She slowly turned away and began to make her way to the hat shop, where she was working as a milliner. Maria arrived at the shop in Gliwice, drained of any feelings, sat down and pondered blankly for a while. She was devoid of any motivation before picking up some fabric and started to make another hat for the shop. The foreboding clouds of war were gathering and the world would be changed forever.

On the train my father's thoughts were nervously circulating through the corridors of his mind with apprehension. Amid the confusion in the moment he was focused on leaving Maria behind, wondering how to survive when confronting the invading German army. Within a short time the sheer force that Poland had to confront from Germany was so overpowering that my father found himself defeated and captured, together with the rest of the soldiers.

On the 18th September 1939 my father was taken Prisoner of War (POW) by the Germans. Regretfully for me, he remained reticent about what happened to him in that prison. Twelve days later he miraculously manged to escape the POW camp on 30th September 1939 and fled into hiding. He never told me how he manged to escape from that prison. Soon after his escape he was re-enlisted into the Polish army.

He was then sent East to fight against the Soviet Union (Russia) on the Soviet front in the region called Wolyn, (Polish: Województwo Wołyńskie), on the borders of Ukraine and the Soviet Union. Poland was under attack by Russia 16 days later on 17th September 1939. Suddenly Poland found herself sandwiched in between two huge aggressors on two fronts in September 1939, and his career as a dentist ultimately never came true. He was gone for many months and taken prisoner by Russia in early March 1940.

As I read the historical facts about that era, I was amazed to learn that during the summer of 1939, negotiations were being conducted with both a British-French group and Germany regarding potential military agreements. To my surprise the Soviet Union chose Germany, which resulted in a German-Soviet agreement on August 19, providing for an exchange of German military and civilian equipment regarding Soviet raw materials. Both countries signed the 'Molotov-Rippentrop Pact' four days later, which contained secret protocols. This Pact divided the states of Northern and Eastern Europe into German and Soviet spheres of influence.

The Polish army was totally unprepared to fight on two fronts against the huge mega powers of Hitler's Germany and Stalin's Soviet Union, which found itself surrounded by Soviet troops and tanks by the thousands in the East. They were simply caught and rounded up as POWs. As a result, the Soviets captured thousands of Polish officers and infantry during their invasion of Poland from the East, and their aim was to wipe out as many Polish officers and soldiers as possible.

They were herded into railroad cattle wagons and transported to the USSR (Union of Soviet Socialist Republics). The plan was to exterminate all the Polish military intelligentsia, as well as all the well-educated Polish citizens. My father was captured in 1940 and loaded onto a cattle train and transported with the rest of the Polish soldiers.

To his disbelief of being captured yet again and facing another POW camp, but this time in Russia, was suspiciously terrifying. My father asked one of the Soviet guards.

"Where are we going to?"

"Smolensk." He replied.

The train journey seemed to be moving towards a dangerous and terrifying destination. The endless monotonous sound of the click-clack clunking of the railway line joints was eerie, as if each click-clack was shortening their time, bringing them closer to an ominous ending in Smolensk. My father had a gut-feeling of great danger if he stayed on the train.

The numbed soldiers silently stared into space where there was no space, gazing at the dim light through the wooden slats at the top of the carriage. As the hours passed away they were wide-eyed with hopelessness on their tired dirty faces, watching a glimmer of day light, which could only be seen flickering through the cracks of the wooden doors of the carriage.

They were all painfully packed in tightly with little room to move about. It was strangely quiet most of the time and the air was filled with an anticipation of fear, as to what awaited them at their destination. The suffocating and gagging stench from human waste, inhumane claustrophobic conditions and forsaken denied dignity was intolerable. Intuitively they all knew they were going to a fateful destiny too horrible to contemplate.

The anxious realization of what will happen to them was urgently terrifying, yet they were numbed and resigned to fate. However, two Polish officers decided to escape from the train with my father. During the night the train journey felt as if their time was coming to an end; already being on Russian soil they had to make a dash for an escape.

My father's heart was racing, pounding with adrenalin, deciding when to open the door and jump. They were all dressed in thick heavy combat uniforms, hoping it would give them some protection when they fell. Suddenly he clutched the door handle and forcefully opened the sliding door. He jumped out of the moving train followed by his two comrades. They fell hard to the ground, rolling down the sloping gravel embankment away from the train line.

Luckily they were not seen by the train guards but were badly bruised and battered by the fall. Lying there in the still of a moonlit night and quiet of the forest, stunned in disbelief that he was out of the train, my father looked at his bleeding hands all cut to shreds from the gravel stones. With pain he wiped his bloodied hands on the front of his uniform. He could still hear the echoing click-clacking of the train in the distance.

In the sudden quiet and dark stillness of night all my father could think of was to survive and yelled to his comrades.

"Hanek, Woytek, are you alright?"

"Yes okay, we have to move and move quickly. Let's go." They replied.

The train continued click-clacking on through the deep forest into silence, but without them, to their relief. They ran and ran as fast as their legs could carry them into the forest and separated, making their own way back to western Poland. As for the rest of all the soldiers and officers on that train, who arrived in Smolensk, they were all placed into a POW camp.

As the days passed by the POW Polish military officers were rounded up on a daily base, put onto another train, caged and taken to Katyn. On arrival they were taken into another building to have their personal identification recorded, plus surrender all their personal items of value. From there they were placed onto buses and driven into the Katyn forest.

Any resistance was futile. The Soviet soldiers forcefully marched them through the forest and made them stand next to a huge pit in the ground. Without any mercy each soldier was welcomed with a Russian bullet through the head and pushed into a mass grave. All those young lives were terminated without sparing any thought of dignity or respect to human life. The mindless atrocities and systematic terror of the extermination program was being carried out in full, under the 'Molotov-Ribbentrop Pact' with agreement by Joseph Stalin.

This war crime became known as "The Katyn Forrest Massacre." The crime was a heinous mass execution of Polish nationals, which was carried out by the People's Commissariat for Internal Affairs (NKVD) in April and May 1940. They were in fact the Soviet secret police. The massacre was approved and proposed by Lavrentiy Beria to execute all members of the Polish Officer Corps and was agreed upon and began from 5th March 1940.

*Josef Stalin and the Soviet Poitburo signed an official document and approved to carry out such a mass killing. The number of victims of this war crime was estimated to be about **22,000** murdered in the Katyn Forrest in Russia, and in the Kalinin and Kharkiv prisons and elsewhere. Among those murdered included the Polish Intelligentsia arrested for allegedly being "intelligence agents, landowners, factory owners, lawyers, saboteurs, gendarmes, officials and priests."*

Indeed 'Stalin' is synonymous with 'Hitler;' even though their ideologies were different. The tyranny of these two insane and very powerful egomaniacs of mass murder was similar and unforgettable. They managed to control the destruction and destiny of millions of people.

Having survived the escape from the train my father trekked very cautiously alone through the countryside across Poland on foot back to Silesia. He was in pain with a bruised body and open wounds to his hands and face, from the fall onto the railway embankment stones. Trying to find some water or a stream in the forest to clean up was not so easy. He was afraid, desperate to survive and enduring gnawing starvation.

Walking to the edge of the forest he saw a lonely distant farmhouse in a field, which had some beetroots and turnips still left over in the ground. Cautiously stepping into the field looking for any sign of people he took some beetroots and started to eat them. As he bit into the beetroot the purple juices were dripping down his hands, chin and on to his uniform, staining his teeth and mouth. Feeling the pangs of starvation he was just frantically gorging himself in desperation with the beetroot.

To stay sane Franus kept thinking of his beloved Maria, in the hope of seeing her again. Black crows in the trees above were watching him and squawking as he looked up into the sky feeling disturbed. The noisy, depressing, ugly and monotonous squawks of the crows irritated him and he felt uncomfortable, making him nervous of being noticed by someone.

He looked at the distant isolated farmhouse again in the quiet of early morning and saw a light through the window. The day was damp, misty, windless, overcast and cold. He spotted an old man in the room who must have been the farm owner. A dog suddenly barked. He was aware that the farmer saw him in the field.

My father was so afraid and fled into the forest to hide. The farmer was also afraid as to who that might be. He grabbed his pitchfork and made his way, following his dog to find that man. Trying to keep up with his dog, the farmer approached the forest and found his dog barking at my father hiding behind some bushes. The famer confronted him and immediately recognised that my father was in a Polish officer's uniform. The farmer was stunned and grabbed him by the arm and said with great urgency.

"You have to get out of here right now. It's too dangerous. Come with me, hurry!"

Being astonished my father said nothing dropping the beetroots and just ran across the muddy field to the farmhouse with him. The farmer saw a totally distressed man from hunger and almost ready to collapse. Afraid of being caught by the Russians again, my father was glad to be in the safety and warmth of the humble farmhouse. Being nervous and a bit out of breath the farmer said.

"I'm Jacek and this is my wife Anna."

With that short introduction Anna quickly ran to the kitchen to get something to eat and drink for my father. He was too starved to even say thank you and gorged the bread and sausage served by Anna.

Jacek told him about the rumours he heard in town the day before, that a few hundred Polish officers were captured and executed in the Katyn Forest area near Smolensk in Russia and that the town was crawling with Russian military. They were both very afraid of the situation and for him.

My father's eyes opened widely with fear and a crushing flow of nausea from a reality too terrifying to accept. He was immediately wondering what might have happened to all the officers and soldiers that were with him on the train, as well as the two officers that escaped with him. He just looked at Jacek and Anna with a face in shock. He went pale with learning such an unimaginable tragedy for all those soldiers.

His eyes looked down at the floor in despair, as his eyes welled up with tears that began dripping down his face onto his clenched hands. The internal turmoil of what had happened to his fellow soldiers and officers was a reality so unbearable, that he just wanted to scream and scream over and over again.

He was hyperventilating from the utter inconceivable sickening insane murderous killing spree that had taken over the human mind. He realized that his plight to get back to Silesia would be fraught with danger. Jacek and Anna were very kind and hospitable to him and told him that he must hide in their house for a while, because there were many Russian soldiers in the area. They fed him and offered him a bed to stay with them until the coast was clear for him to keep going west.

This was the first sleep he would have had since jumping from the train in Russia. He felt so lucky to come across such good people to help him. He was thanking god for his intuition and escaping from the train of death to Katyn. Jacek and Anna cared for him for two days. He was given some old farmer's clothes and told to get out of his uniform, as it was much too dangerous to be seen in a Polish army uniform and Anna suggested destroying it.

My father gave his uniform to Jacek and changed into the old farmers clothes, looking like a peasant farmer. Jacek placed the uniform into the fireplace, which was in the living room. As my father watched his uniform slowly burning his heart sank; he stared at the smouldering smoke rising into the chimney and observed his uniform disappearing, as if his identity as a Polish officer was being slowly extinguished into oblivion. Jacek and Anna were heartbroken upon seeing what was happening to their disintegrating army and to Poland. The silence in the room was almost choking the three of them with grief.

Lamentably my father looked at the ashes in the fireplace. His internal heartfelt sentiment with his uniform was vanishing with the smoke of an unidentifiable person, who no longer existed anymore; which was also happening to Poland, being systematically and politically consumed into the ashes of her two plunderers at the same time.

In grief for his country he left the farm with gratitude for the kindness and understanding of Jacek and Anna, never to forget them. They gave him a warm coat, bread and sausages to survive for a few days and sent him on his way with many hugs and a loving prayer for his safety. He looked at them for the last time, turned away and left in tears.

The constant struggle to keep moving was like being in a relentless exhausting flight mode within his mind and veins. The forests of Poland are home to many wild boar, wolves and bears to be avoided, as they can be dangerous. In his mind he was feeling so vulnerable to all those natural elements, but mostly the German infantry, who overran Poland as he moved further west. He avoided towns and villages, hiding on his way in the forests, which are vast and plentiful in Poland.

It gave him protection and the chance to eat anything edible, such as wild nuts and occasional vegetables, still found in the ground on some farms. His wounds began to heal after washing his hands at the farmhouse where he found shelter. Every sound, movement, animal, the wind rustling dead leaves and blowing through the tree branches, every change of light, like dancing shadows in the night, made him pensive, alert and frightened.

He was in the endless mode of a trembling bird alert to danger, like a wild dear being stalked by a lion and ready to run. The pitch black of night, with cloudy skies, was a frightening endurance needing nerves as strong as steel. Even the sound of an owl on the moonlit nights was ghostly. At least on bright moonlit nights, with a clear sky, gave him the chance to move on further to Silesia.

As the Soviet Army took over from the East, many Polish military were forced into a Soviet uniform. Poland was left totally defenceless and slowly engulfed into submission to Stalin. Miraculously my father survived from becoming a casualty of the Katyn Massacre. Poland was left alone to defend herself and suffered the consequences of a total Russian occupation in the end. There was no help from the allied forces coming to their rescue from the West. Yet Poland fought with the allied forces outside Poland for the freedom of their countries, but was left forsaken when Poland needed help.

This mass murder and atrocity committed by the Soviets in Katyn was blamed on the Germans, through a well-organized and ruthless propaganda machine, denying the truth. All the Poles knew that it was a lie but could do nothing about it. If any Polish military person or civilian questioned the real truth of Katyn they were swiftly dealt with, and again without mercy.

My father was always under the illusion that about 700 Polish officers were executed in Katyn. He heard rumours that it was a few thousand, but never lived long enough to learn the truth that the figure was in fact 22,000 Polish officers and soldiers combined, who were executed and dumped into a mass grave.

I learnt about this mass murder with astonishment and shock while watching TV about a flight from Warsaw to Smolensk. That flight was carrying members of the Polish government and crashed on landing in Smolensk near Katyn on the 10th April 2010. All 96 people aboard along with President Lech Kaczyński and his wife Maria, with the president's entire cabinet were killed. They were on their way to commemorate the 70th anniversary of the loss of all those lives slaughtered in Katyn in 1940. The Russian President, Vladimir Putin, was waiting for them to give an official apology to Poland for the massacre. It never happened or was in truth not even intended, as the focus was on the tragedy of that forsaken flight. Sabotage was suspected, but never proven and Katyn was yet again left forgotten in the modern history of the 21st century.

It took my father a long time to get back to Silesia. All he could think of was to survive with his willpower to be with his beloved Maria and in her loving arms again. When he finally arrived in Silesia he was exhausted, hungry, battered, looking unshaved and emaciated. He made his way trembling frantically, knowing the danger of being in German territory again. He managed to keep hidden until he reached his home town of Mikolow with relief.

The fear of arrest by the Germans, who still occupied the region, was nerve-wrecking. Monotonously, step by step he kept going in fear, so very aware of each step and sound he cautiously made, hoping to find Maria at her address in Podlesie. His mind was occupied with determined survival and faith believing she was alive. He felt like he was entering into a den of hungry lions ready to pounce on him.

It was late evening and the diminishing light was already growing into darkness. The sky was bleak and cloudy with a damp gently falling drizzle. He was hiding in some bushes nearby close to the road and a bus stop. He cautiously began to walk down the street, looking behind him to make sure it was safe from German soldiers when he suddenly saw a woman getting off a bus.

She was dressed in an elegant smart and sharp stylish dark brown woollen coat, with flat wide box-like shoulder lapels and a classic velure maroon coloured hat. He saw her in the dim light of a street lamp and intuitively felt that the woman looked like his beloved Maria. She was returning home from work in the nearby town of Gleiwitz/Gliwice. Suddenly recognising her, my father was so elated, his heart racing and almost in tears, his face radiant as he slowly ran to her, struggling in a very low voice calling out:

"Maria, Maria dearest, my darling."

On hearing his familiar voice she turned her head in disbelief and stared into his eyes, her face looking shocked to see him after almost seven months. She was overwhelmed with joy on seeing him, opening her loving arms and tightly holding him, not wanting to let him go.

Keeping her voice low not to attract any attention, Maria stepped back to look at him properly and her heart sank on seeing Franus in such a dreadful state, yet overwhelmed to see him. She was saying.

"Franus, my loving Franus. I don't believe it. Thank god you're alive. My god! Franus what are you doing here?

"Maria, German soldiers are everywhere and we might be arrested if they find me." Franus said urgently.

"What on earth happened to you?" Maria asked.

"I'll tell you later. I must hide" Franus said.

Maria instinctively sensed the terrifying thought of being caught and arrested for being with a Polish officer. It was already dark as they walked towards her flat in the drizzle, staring into each other's eyes.

He just kept looking at her, as the drizzle was settling on her face and hair. The delicate make-up on her face with rich red lipstick made her look radiant. Her familiar perfume was suddenly piercing Franus's nostrils, dulling his senses into oblivion, with the great love of his life in his arms and nothing mattered in that moment. Maria's wet face was stroked by Franus, touching her beautiful lips and fondling her rich dark chestnut coloured hair, Franus was in heaven in the void of time. The war meant nothing momentarily and her tears of joy were unstoppable and streaming down her cheeks saying.

"I'm so afraid for you. Let's hurry." Maria said.

Their urgency to survive was paramount. They arrived at the flat in Podlesie, both were bewildered to be together and alive. The situation of mixed emotions of joy and fear permeated their existence from now on. He told Maria what happened to him at the Soviet front and about the mass executions in Katyn, which he briefly heard about from Jacek on his journey back to Silesia. She was horrified and grateful that he escaped and survived.

However, being very Catholic they felt awkward being together in the small one bed-sit flat together for the first time. My parents, especially my mother was awkward, feeling that their courtship was so suddenly abruptly ended and forced into togetherness that they never experienced before. My father understood that this situation was uncomfortable and improper for Maria, even though their circumstances were abnormal.

Looking at each other, smiling and chatting, they realized that their long engagement was over. They decided to quickly get married while they could, in case it might be too late.

They organised their marriage hastily at the local church. There was no reception or any wedding celebrations of any kind. All they wanted was to become husband and wife. Nothing else mattered.

THE TRIPLE SOLDIER And My Mother

He married Maria Malgorzata Superniok, on 25th March 1940 in Mikolow, in the main Catholic Church in town. From there they started life as best as they could. Maria became Maria Faron and eventually my mother. They managed to have only one wedding photo as a keepsake for their eventual children in the future. I can only imagine the joy and happiness my parents had and relieved to be finally married.

My mother soon became pregnant with her first child. Suddenly the fear of what might happen to both of them was unthinkable. Knowing that hiding from the Gestapo forever was not possible, as it would soon be found out. My father wore new civilian clothes, which my mother bought for him, hoping to stay in disguise for as long he could. However, their hidden private world of love and secret existence was doomed. They were living in a world of fear and cocooned surreal happiness, knowing it was just a momentary fantasy.

My father stayed in Silesia for a short while in blissful union with his beloved wife. Even though he survived execution in Katyn his destiny was soon to dramatically change. The day eventually arrived for him, when there was a strong banging on the door of their flat one late evening. It was already dark and Maria nervously opened the door knowing it could be the Gestapo. To their horror and fatal expectation two German soldiers stood there and asked in German.

"Good evening. Where's the Polish soldier you're hiding? We know he's here. You're both under arrest."

Maria felt ill, her legs going to jelly, the blood draining from her head and almost fainting from fear. With that confrontation there was no argument or escape. The tension and fear of possible execution terrified them.

They both kept their cool concealing any fear. My father came to the door and spoke in perfect German.

"Yes, I'm the soldier you want. She is my wife so please let her go."

"No, she is also under arrest. You have five minutes to collect your papers and come with us. Be quick! The Gestapo is waiting to meet you." The soldier said.

My parents were driven to a very large and beautiful house in town, dated from the 18th century, to meet the Gestapo, who was a tall and very direct, heavy looking middle aged man with total confidence about what he wanted. The office was elegantly decorated and adorned with the Nazi flag and a photo of their Fuehrer, Adolf Hitler, was hanging on the wall near the Gestapo's desk. They were greeted with an insincere smile of despotism.

They were seated in front of him in plush black leather chairs. Internally shaking with fear during the interrogation session, which lasted two hours; both of them were almost resigned to be sentenced to face either the firing squad or Auschwitz. However, speaking fluent German was to be a great asset in saving both of them.

Under the German Flag:

After being interrogated my father was congratulated by the Gestapo on his well-educated spoken German language. He was impressed by him and then stood up and said.

"Herrn Faron, you will be enlisted into our labour camps. Welcome to The Third Reich, go and collect your 'Work Book' (Arbeitsbuch) and papers as you will be leaving for work right away. As for you, Frau Faron you're free to go. Heil Hitler!"

He said, standing up and loyally stretching out his right arm.

The situation was so abrupt, cold blooded, sudden, brutally heartless and so matter of fact. They could do nothing to oppose such a decision by the Gestapo since he was now the law.

My father was forcibly used into working for some German companies, like many other Polish men, who were also forced to do so in the region. Many of them never returned home and died of malnutrition and exhaustion. That was my father's greatest fear for himself and most of all for leaving Maria a widow.

As my father was leaving the room to collect his work papers and uniforms, his thoughts were almost blank. He stared at Maria with a stunned expression of painful and fearful grief letting her know, with his comforting loving smile, how much he loved her.

My mama was almost immobilized to make a move and leave the room until a soldier escorted her out of the office. As she stood up and walked away from the room she was dazed with what had just happened. Unable to comprehend that in only two hours she was without her husband, and the love of her life was disappearing into thin air, crippling and numbing her mind.

They met outside the room in the corridor for a brief moment to say goodbye. The hearts of my parents in this moment crumbled into an inner refusal to accept such an unbelievable turn of events, which rocked the very foundations of their souls.

In a frantic moment, knowing that Maria was pregnant, and wanting to be remembered in his family, Franus held her shoulders in desperation. Trying to appear strong for his wife and looking almost speechless he said.

"Maria, when you have our baby. If it's a boy name him Walter. If it's a girl name her Sofia. Don't worry I'll be fine. Just take care of yourself and our baby. I love you."

With that last request he had to go. He turned around, walked away and was gone. He felt as if he was struck by a lightning bolt and totally stunned with what happened.

Mama was allowed to go home since her husband was now working for the Nazi regime, not knowing where he was going to be sent. With such a climax of daunting surrealism that took place, neither Maria nor her Franus would have ever contemplated such a twisted turn of events in the war. They were both in shock not even being allowed to say goodbye properly.

In August 1942 my mother received a letter from her husband written entirely in German, letting her know that he was conscripted into the Wehrmacht on 25th July 1942 in Breslau (Wroclaw). He signed his letter as Franz. Why didn't he write in Polish? She wondered?

These changing situations for my father to obey orders, contrary to his Polish loyalties, must have been internally torturous, explosive and insane to endure. On reading his letter mama was drained and lost with what took place, as if her beloved Polish officer no longer existed and was thrown into another sphere.

How was this possible for her to now be the wife of a German soldier? It was unthinkable and unacceptable for her to understand

and believe. Polish was not allowed to be spoken or used in Breslau at the time and was punishable if caught.

In Silesia many former citizens were from the Second Polish Republic from across the Polish territories annexed by Nazi Germany. Following the German invasion of Poland many Polish soldiers were forcibly conscripted into the Garman army (Wehrmacht) in Upper Silesia and in Pomerania. The Third Reich considered them as German citizens and therefore subject to drumhead court-martial in case of draft evasion. The author, professor Ryszard Kaczmarek of the university of Silesia in Katowice wrote a monograph titled 'Polacy w Wehrmachcie,' "Poles in the Wehrmacht".

He noted the scale of this phenomenon, which was much larger than previously assumed, because 90% of the inhabitants of these western regions of pre-war Poland were ordered to register as Germans. It was also known, as the Nazi Deutsche Volksliste by the invader regardless of a person's will. The number of conscripts is not fully understood, which remains an unknown enigma. However, in 1946 the British Secretary for War estimated that between 60,000 to 69,000 men were captured by the Allies and the British in North-West Europe. The overwhelming majority in the Polish army, which my father originally was, re-enlisted into the Polish Army under British Command after capture and were processed about their true identity. Many of the Polish Armed forces under British Command ended up serving in the West against the Germans until the end of WWII.

History does not mention much about this situation, which needs to be understood why it happened to my father, regarding being conscripted into the German army. Thousands of men in the Polish army ended up in the same situation.

This situation could be well argued as to what is right or wrong. On the Soviet front many Polish soldiers ended up in Soviet uniforms, and eventually all of them did, as the Soviets took over the entire nation of Poland. Likewise, those on the German front, many Polish soldiers ended up in German uniforms. Should a human being remain loyal and patriotic to their country and gladly surrender themselves to be executed? Or, should one be loyal to try and survive and be there for their family? I beg the question for you be the judge.

Suddenly my father was in the German army, serving The Third Reich and Hitler. I stepped into the footsteps of my father and felt his anguish asking myself how it might have felt. To who was he supposed to be loyal or patriotic and obey orders?

His former fellow Polish soldiers and comrades instantly became his enemy, when he was in a German uniform. The dilemma of right and wrong, friend or foe, loyalty without choice, just obeying orders, who to shoot to kill and who was really his enemy? That would have been the biggest ludicrous contradictory difficulties for my father.

His mind would have been in tormented turmoil; feeling so trapped and forced to listen to the nationalistic and patriotic propaganda thrust upon him by the very oppressor and enemy when in a Polish uniform. Then forced to silently obey his enemy would have been a torture of his soul. I cannot envisage such a shocking circumstance; yet it happened to him.

He had to live and survive such a paradox of ideologies; it would have been inconceivable. I fully understand why my father was reluctant to talk about that part of his experiences in a German uniform. It was evident to me that his tortured mind of that part of his life was being buried into the deepest chasms of his heart and soul. All the allied forces were his friend when in a Polish uniform, but in a German uniform they were his enemy. How does one deal with this to stay sane and normal? It must have plagued my father for the rest of his life.

Between 1942 and 1943, my father was sent to join the German forces with the occupation of Holland, as a German soldier. Time was moving fast through the advancing brutality and insanity of war. My father stepped into a church in Vissingen, Holland. He sat alone in a pew in front of the altar and knelt in prayer. He looked at the Christ on the cross and went into deep silence wondering how all this madness will end.

Scouring his heart, contemplating if he would ever see his wife again and if he would ever see his unknown baby, was difficult to imagine and believe that it would happen one day. He clenched his hands and closed his eyes, deeply in sadness with despair about the war and his situation. His mind held on to the image of his wife, as if he was daydreaming of being in another misty world, seeing the memories when they were together, where only love and happiness existed. A priest saw him and came to talk with him for a while.

The priest sat next to him and saw the pain showing on his face and compassionately looked into his soul. My father told the priest that he wanted to see his wife and unknown child in Poland so badly. This priest listened to his broken heart about what happened to him, smiled and gave him a relic of the "Martyrs of Gorki," (Dutch martyrs of the 17th. century). He told him to carry that relic with him all the time and that he would eventually be reunited with his wife and child again. He gave my father the 'hope' he needed in the moment, which gave him great strength and he kept that relic in his pocket throughout the war and beyond.

On one particular occasion, when I was a teenager, my father showed me that relic, which was a small bone encased in a circular brass container with a glass cover. My mother told me that the relic eventually brought them together. Luckily he managed to get a short furlough to see his wife and child once, when his child was about two years and eight months old in 1943, before leaving Holland for the war front in northern Italy. Even German soldiers needed to be with their loved ones, as every soldier does.

Obeying orders, my father just went along with wherever he was sent to. The war continued and eventually he was separated from the soldiers he knew in Holland and sent to northern Italy. Another duty was presented to him, making him feel nothing more than the pawn in a game of chess. Just being another dispensable number without any human value, but a useful bullet carrier to kill for the fatherland of Germany. I will never know how he might have felt living through such insanity and trying to stay normal.

My father was pushed from place to place, starting with Antwerp in Belgium from late 1942 and on to Vissingen in Holland from November 1942 to June 1943. Later on the alliance between Germany and Italy broke down under German occupied Italy and my father was sent to Ferrara in July 1943. He told me that he also spent time in La Spezia from August to November 1943, which he loved and where he learnt a great deal of the Italian language.

He was later transported to the area of Fiume Sangro, Province of Chieti in Italy, where he faced the "Battle of Sangro" against the Western Allies. He mentioned that the weather was steadily worsening, producing miserable conditions for those who had to live out in the open. He told me about the rising water in the river, the mud, the rubble, the rain, the cold and the struggle in the terrible conditions that surrounded him, as well as the Allied Forces.

Field Marshal Montgomery's 8th Army in Italy was, just as it had been in the Desert, a multinational organisation. Now some old Desert veterans, the 2nd New Zealand Division, known simply as the 'Div' amongst New Zealanders, re-joined the fray in Italy. By the 28th November the skies cleared. This was the moment when the attack on the Germans started, who were entrenched on the other side of the river, surrounded by barren hills. The entire Kiwi division moved into line to cross the Sangro River. The skies lit up with lightning flashes and the thundering roar of exploding ammunition was echoing in the surrounding treeless high country.

He told me that during that battle he was shooting into the sky (God's window, as told by him), presumably because he did not want to kill any Allied Soldiers, since his sympathies were always with the Allies, which Poland was a part of. He faced the 2nd New Zealand Division in the attack across the Sangro River. After the fierce battle, which lasted all night, the Allied Army regiment surrounded the Germans.

The noise of gun fire and exploding grenades was dying away at dawn. After the battle, the silence, the dead and the groaning of the injured was unbearable. Deep in his soul he felt that all life was precious, regardless of what uniform you were in. The Allied Army took all of them as Prisoners of War and among them was my father. He was relieved to be in the hands of his Allies, grateful in his heart to the New Zealanders for saving his life by default. With a strained face he looked at me, stopped talking, unable to continue any further.

I often wonder how many soldiers managed to recover after a war experience that my father had to endure. I have no doubt that many soldiers would have been totally broken psychologically for many years after the war.

The 2nd New Zealand Division's first two months of combat in Italy had left some 1600 men dead or wounded. The morale of the surviving troops was significantly lowered by these loses, as well as the intense cold, the prevailing sense of failure and the recognition that progress over the rugged terrain was going to be slow. God knows how many German and Italian soldiers also perished in the aftermath.

Under the British flag:

After rounding up all the prisoners he was then shipped to North Africa, along with all of the remaining German and Italian soldiers and placed into a large POW camp in Tunisia. The sea voyage to Tunisia was a tight and cramped situation for all the prisoners. However, they were not destined for a mass slaughter, as he would have faced during his train journey to Katyn. This time the British were his saviour and a better chance to survive.

Being reticent about his experiences in the POW camp, he mentioned the extreme Spartan conditions and the cold at night in the tent. When waking up in the morning he had to break a thin sheet of ice to wash in a bucket of water. Yet the days were hot and dry, which was a new experience for him being in the desert for the first time.

The camp was filled with thousands of prisoners from Italy and Germany. It was in the POW camp that the British sorted out all the Poles, who were forced to serve in the German army. Therefore my father was reinstated with the Allies. With his nature he would have made some friends when in the German army. Ironically the German soldiers were now the prisoners and he was their eventual captor, being an ally with the British. Suddenly the Germans were his enemy again.

They later shipped all the Poles to The United Kingdom in Scotland. Once in Falkirk, Scotland he was enlisted into the Polish

Forces under British command. The sea voyage took quite a few days to get to Scotland. Miraculously my father was alive and now wondering about what new events he would have to face under the British. However, he felt much safer with the British allied forces since leaving Poland, rather than serving in the German army.

After landing in Scotland he was placed into another POW camp and life took on another surprising twist that he never expected. With effect from 29.03.1944 he was given a new identity, under the assumed name of Franciszek MICHOROWSKI and was posted to 3 Supply Company, 1st Armoured Division, and 1st Polish Corps on 09.04.1944. He was given a British uniform, yet again wondering and questioning who his enemy was this time.

The British issued counterfeit military papers bearing false names and made all of them a contingent of the Allied Polish Army and part of the British army. The reason my father, (Franz Faron in the German army), and all his fellow comrades were given false names and counterfeit documents, was to make sure that they would not be identified as ex-German soldiers, in case of capture; otherwise they would have been executed by firing squad as traitors.

My father was given a British uniform with his rank of 2nd Lieutenant and sent to Normandy, France. Listening to his story, as to what happened to him, left me speechless with amazement that he survived so many traumas and changes of uniforms when serving for three countries. It was bewildering for me to comprehend his endurance and how many other people during the war also managed to survive the most unthinkable situations.

I admired him and wanted to know more and more about his experiences, which became too painful for him to speak about most of the time, making him suddenly silent unable to continue. He was reluctant to go there and relive the war all over again. There were times when I felt his pain and it showed on his face when he could no longer go on telling me his story. He would just stop and remain silent.

Andrew Faron

MY FATHER'S NEW IDENTITY 29.03.1944

POLISH ARMY

SOLDIER'S NAME AND DESCRIPTION

Cpl. Cadet FARON
Name (in Capitals) MICHOROWSKI
Christian Names (in full) FRANCISZEK
Date of Birth 27.9.1913
Place of Birth:
- Parish Gródek Jagielloński Orzesze
- In or near the town of Brzezyna
- In the county of Poland

Trade on Enlistment clerk

Nationality of Father at Birth Polish
Nationality of Mother at Birth Polish
Religious denomination R.C.
Photographed Number 34168
Signature of Soldier Michorowski Franciszek
Date

DESCRIPTION ON ENLISTMENT

Height ft. 167 cm. Weight 61 kg. Lbs.
Maximum Chest ins. Complexion
Eyes Hair
Distinctive Marks and Minor Defects

P/12155 Dokonano poprawek wpisów
K.U. Nr. 1. L. dz. 3510/44 N/46

24

Today I have a deeper understanding with the veteran soldiers, who served in Vietnam, and now with the current wars in Iraq, Afghanistan and Syria etc. They are also unable to deal with their shocking war experiences, which has left many of them emotionally traumatised.

AUSTRALIA 1973: My Father's 60th Birthday in Fiji:

At that time we already lived in Australia. My father was a man of many talents. He bought himself a modest set of tiny instruments with which to repair watches, and enjoyed repairing them for people as a hobby. He was fascinated with watches and always spoke about them especially Patek Philippe, Omega and Longines Swiss watches, which were his love. He also had a wish to visit a south Pacific Island once in his life.

It was his 60th Birthday and for a gift I gave him a Longines Watch with an air ticket to Fiji for a holiday with me for ten days. He was taken aback so much that he could hardly speak when he received my gift. As for the ticket to Fiji, it was simply a dream come true, which he never expected in his life. Then he opened the box with the watch in it and just looked at me with disbelief. Words were not needed and the utter delight on his face was my pleasure and gift of love to him, rather than the other way round.

He took a deep breath and with a breaking voice holding back tears, he hugged me and said: *("Dzeinkuje ci bardzo Jedrus z calego serca, jaki wspanialy prezent - zaniemowilem");* "Thank you so very much Andrew from all my heart, what an incredible present, I'm speechless"

With a big smile gently shaking his head he said: *("Co za niespodzianka!").*

"What an unexpected surprise!"

He was speechless for a while, and a few days later we flew on a Pan Am Jumbo Jet to Fiji.

As the aircraft lifted off the runway I saw him tightly grab onto the arm rest in astonishment and fright, to be in flight for the very first time. Once at cruising altitude he looked out of the window at the clouds in amazement and said.

"I can't work out which is the sky or the ocean." I just smiled at him.

We were together alone, father and son, for the very first time in our lives. I got to know him better and loved being with him, as we went to see many places in Fiji.

He was like a child for the first time, forgetting the past harshness during his childhood, the war in Europe and his exiled life in London. I hired a car and we travelled inland to the highlands of Fiji whereupon we came by small villages, which were an eye opener regarding poverty in comparison to Australia. Here my father's compassionate and magnanimous nature suddenly appeared to surface, as a surprise to me, since we had never been in this situation before.

He wanted to spend a bit more time with these people, who were so open hearted and generous in hospitality. The true value of my father's loving heart would deeply touch my soul far more than I would have ever imagined possible of him in the future.

The natives offered some local fruit to us on a banana leaf and sang Fijian songs. My father was deeply touched and warmly enchanted by them. In the South Pacific the native people sing innocently from their heart, which is a rather nostalgic memory for me. The experience for us was a very special memory to cherish, especially for me, as such experiences with my father would never be repeated again.

He was so relaxed on this timeless tropical Fijian paradise. My father was enchanted with the beauty of the coconut palm forest, which swept down to the powdery white sandy beach and crystal clear water of a peaceful lagoon. We enjoyed a day on a coral atoll with the locals and had a wonderful private time in the seclusion of a South Pacific dream.

I was twenty seven years old by then, sitting quietly with my father enjoying a cocktail, listening to the distant surf crashing on the coral reef. I observed my father deep in thought. He was sitting under a coconut palm in a reclusive area, staring at the beach, with his drink of rum and coke in his hand. I disturbed him and asked him what he was thinking about.

He calmly looked at me and began to talk, with a deep breath and a little stutter, about that shocking day landing on the beaches in the Battle of Normandy, with the supply materiel.

THE TRIPLE SOLDIER And My Mother

FATHER AND SON 1973

MY FATHER AT A SMALL VILLAGE WITH THE NATIVES IN FIJI

ANDREW AND FRANCISZEK FARON ON A BOAT CRUISE IN FIJI

It was here, in the peaceful and undisturbed moments alone with my father that I listened to an unspeakable war experience, when he met a German soldier in the Battle of Normandy. I am so grateful that my father shared that one unforgettable encounter in France, which was so traumatic that it left me shattered. I did not know what to say to him. I just gave him a heartfelt compassionate hug with tears.

I believe that my father never intended to tell that story to anyone, but somehow he found the courage to tell me. I regret that my father did not impart more information to me, as to his war experiences, but I knew he could not talk about them any further.

He was reticent about that part of his life and most probably wanted to forget the painful memories, and avoid reliving the trauma by talking about it. I am certain there was a great deal left untold. I was so grateful to him for what he did tell me and am so proud of my father's courage and ability to survive the Battle of Normandy, in spite of the massive human carnage the battle inflicted.

The Battle of Normandy, 6th June 1944.

The invasion of Normandy took place under the command of General Dwight D. Eisenhower. The first phase of the invasion was D-Day. My father was in a later phase, with all the supply divisions, carrying the materiel from England, under the British flag, in which my father took part from 1st August 1944. The hostilities continued in Europe and the supply divisions from England kept up with the pace of advancement, until the invasion and hostilities ceased on 7th May 1945. After that the occupation and rezoning of Germany took place.

It was the 1st August 1944, hot and sunny, with a calm sea on approach to the beach. The soldiers were in the amphibious landing crafts, in full combat uniform and ready to face the 'German' enemy. Everyone was in an alert mode full of adrenalin pumping through their veins, fearful of what they were about to confront. It was as if descending into a hell of total nightmarish inconceivable horror beyond description or any understanding!

My father described his landing on the beaches of Normandy

carrying the supplies. Upon seeing the human carnage, the stench of death, rotting bodies floating in the water, blood and slaughter surrounding him, he was distraught.

Countless bodies dismembered, with bits and pieces of human remains scattered everywhere on the beach and inland shocked him, causing nausea wanting to vomit. He rushed all the supplies to where they were needed amid all the exploding grenades, rifle firing and more dead bodies, it was terrifying. He was in hell; 'Dante's Inferno' was unleashed everywhere, as he made his way inland day by day to Caen, until he was faced with opposition by the German army.

Suddenly he was confronted by a tired dirty faced German soldier, hiding alone in a pit of rubble around him and pointing a rifle at him shaking with fear. For a moment time stood still and an eerie silence prevailed, like being in an empty time warp. He was in shock and rigid, unable to move upon seeing this solitary German soldier staring at him. He could not shoot in the confusion of friend or foe.

He was in a vacuum of time, numbed with a strange feeling of being in slow motion. He had a momentary flashback seeing his German army comrades. To his astonishment this soldier was a familiar face. In his mind, another flashback memory, he could see himself sharing a beer, laughing, eating pretzels and telling jokes with him. He recognised him; it was Jürgen, with whom he had spent time during the occupation of Holland. Time stopped! He was facing turmoil in his explosive thoughts.

"Oh my god, how could this be happening to me at a moment where I have to kill a friend or spare his life? God help me!"

He could remember how they talked about their wives and child in a bar in Vissingen and Jürgen showing him the locket next to his heart, with a photo of his wife and son. All they wanted was to go home after the war was over. He struggled with being trapped in time and tried to get out of that strange inter-dimensional vacuum. In choking, heart palpitating desperation, confusion and tremor, he shouted out in German.

"Jürgen, Jürgen don't shoot, don't shoot, It's me, Franz. Stay where you are."

My father stood there paralysed in helpless shock on hearing a rifle shot echoing in his ears. With the sudden smell of gun powder, in that moment an allied bullet shot Jürgen in the heart and he watched him instantly fall in death with his eyes open. Jürgen's locket with the photo of his wife and son was opened next to his heart covered in blood. My father was rigid, staring and staring at Jürgen's bleeding body unable to feel anything more than shock. Time instantly went at high speed to move on.

In my father's mind his soul was screaming and going mad with shock and outrage.

"No, no, no, oh god no; what have you done? This is not happening. My god, my god, what have we all done? Why, why, why? This is insane, this is all insane. Stop it, stop it!" Crumbling inside with a breaking heart, like a grenade exploding in his brain.

What would have gone through my father's mind at that moment is too terrifying to even try and imagine or feel? His heart was shattered like a grenade exploding inside him and he had to keep moving on with all the other soldiers, concealing his emotions, feeling shocked, traumatized and ready to scream.

"Keep moving, keep moving now! Move on, move, move hurry!" He heard the orders.

In a split second his friend, who survived for so long was fatally shot in front of him. A soldier and a 'friend' he fought alongside in a German uniform that was in the wrong place at the wrong time. Jürgen was nothing more than just another dispensable victim of war. No time to mourn, no funeral or any sermon and priest for this man's slaughter, except leaving behind a memory and an inconsolable grieving heart by his wife and family.

There was no sense to be made from such an incomprehensible moment, except the questioning of a world gone mad. There was no time to grieve or be sentimental and sad except to keep moving on. Allowing yourself any loving emotion of grieving was disallowed. On and on they moved with the rest of the soldiers, who were already delirious from the situation beyond any sense of understanding why they were even there, killing people for whom and why. No wonder, soldiers in battle zones cannot recover as easily as we think.

My father stopped talking, looked into my eyes and said.

"I'm disgusted with what humanity is capable of doing."

The shock for him was so terrible and over powering. He shook his head, looked up into the deep blue sky above and held back his tears. He did not say anything more to me about that experience ever again. I cannot even imagine what it would have been like to find one's friend in the wrong uniform, in the wrong place and in the wrong time during a battle.

My heart went out to him with a deep love and compassion about his terrible memories of the war years. I was speechless and just held his hand with tears in my heart. I could not even dare to imagine what my father endured. The casualties of that battle were staggering. It is estimated that over 425,000 Allied and German troops were killed, wounded or went missing during the Battle of Normandy. This figure includes over 209,000 Allied casualties, with nearly 37,000 dead amongst the ground forces and a further 16,714 deaths amongst the Allied air forces.

One comment my father once told me was interesting. When he was with the German army, all they wanted was to go home and be with their families; no different than the Polish or British soldiers. They lost the plot of why they were even there in the first place.

He also admired the British military, with their patience and calmness, being able to make a cup of tea in the trenches, amidst the surrounding chaos and confusion of war. There was a humane side to every soldier no matter who they were. How amazing that my father's life was saved by British allied forces and managed surviving in the service of three different armies, as well as the Battle of Normandy.

My father felt uncomfortable and embarrassed about being in the German Army and it was kept as a family secret until I was old enough to understand. Some Polish people referred to the Silesians as Germans and double-sided semi traitors, which was due to the shifting German border in Silesia's political history. In this matter there is no blame game or accusations and judgments to be made, as he was, like many thousands, a victim of the war.

I felt sad for him and gave him a big hug, telling him that it was all a long time ago and that I loved him. His story is one that was too difficult to talk about, due to the delicate nature of the subject and the situation in which so many Polish soldiers in Silesia were trapped in, without a choice. In the end one wonders: Who is your enemy?

For my father there were no enemies. What an outcome of fate! It was all a question of survival to get back with your loved ones, when the insanity of war was over. After what he told me I fully understood why he never spoke about it again. His pain of the war experience was one he kept silently and deeply buried in his heart. I have also kept silent about it until now. Having been in a Polish uniform and later in a German uniform and suddenly in a British uniform, gave him an insight into all the three nations rather unexpectedly. He amazingly kept enduring 'the twisted net' of war games thrust onto him.

My father did his very best to survive for his family and loved ones. He suffered the trauma of war for the rest of his life and was a hero in my eyes. Most importantly for me was that he was my loving father.

Such an experience gave him a very rare insight and point of view, of what and 'who really is the enemy.' It was something he questioned in his heart for the rest of his life. Once again my father was in a third uniform, but this time a British one. The question of patriotic loyalties yet again became an issue. Who is the enemy, became the big question, 'friend or foe?' His fellow Polish comrades in Polish uniform were again his 'friend' and the comrades in German uniform were his 'foe.'

This insane situation remained a paradox in his heart forever, realizing that all enemies are only according to the ruling power you are serving under. The enemy is what you are forced to accept according to the uniform of the nation you serve.

My father lamented about the entire madness of the war and was glad he survived. But for him the real truth was that enemies are created and in reality we are all friends. As a result Nationalism and Patriotism left him cold. He had a magnanimous nature and did his best to keep going and make the best of what he had left to live with. He had no enemies and accepted all good people he came in contact with.

I once asked my father, as an adult, to imagine if every soldier was naked, how would you know who to shoot? He looked at me with a surprised questioned look on his face, then smiled with a chuckle and said.

"Good question; obviously that is why we are forced to wear a uniform, otherwise we all look the same."

Yes, precisely, we are all the same and yet why are we forced to kill each other? Isn't that amazing?

> *"The pioneers of a warless world are the young who refuse to join the armed forces."*
> – Albert Einstein.

I ask myself if all that death was necessary to win or lose the game for both sides. Nobody has ever told me that it was a good thing, but there are those who say that it was necessary to end the war. Have we evolved enough not to repeat such a slaughter again? The answer is NO. The same war games continue on our TV screens daily.

His absence from my mother turned from months into years and by September 1944 my mama received a telegram from the German War Office that he was listed as 'Missing in Action.' However, my father had no knowledge of the bad news my mother had received.

My father was missing in action but not dead. He survived the execution of a Russian bullet in Katyn in the Polish uniform, then with the German forces in a German uniform in Italy, and eventually the Battle of Normandy in a British uniform.

By then Poland was already under the occupation of Russia, The Soviet Union. Overnight communism reigned over Poland and once again all the citizens of Poland were enduring a new regime, but this time under the tyranny of Stalin.

Poland was unable to defend herself against two massive powers, attacking her from the West by Germany and from the East by Russia, like two hyenas attacking her from the left and the right at once. What lay ahead for ravaged Poland, which was being ripped apart between an unfortunate political duel between Germany and The Soviet Union, became a tragedy? Such political games weighed heavily on the already damaged psyche of an emotionally destroyed nation. Poland was abandoned by the Western Allies in WWII towards the end of the war.

Then three very powerful statesmen, Winston Churchill, Franklin D Roosevelt and Joseph Stalin, made decisions at the famous Yalta Conference in 1945, Crimea, and signed off Poland to Stalin. The Polish nation felt forgotten and betrayed.

It is amazing for me that such decisions continue to be currently made, by just a few leaders in our world today, simply by the stroke of a pen. It seems to be almost unbelievable and yet it is true! Poland was an ally of the west, and fought against German and Soviet oppression.

My father told me that the Poles had not forgiven Churchill, who remains a traitor to Poland, for what happened to Poland after the communist takeover in 1945. After aiding the Allies with experienced soldiers throughout the war, with divisions like the Polish 2nd Corps and Polish 1st Armored Division in Normandy, Poland was given over to Russia, The Soviet Union, without a fight.

'The pen is mightier than the sword, 1839'
– Edward Bulwer Lytton.

As a result of such betrayal, 'The Rape of Poland' lasted over 50 years of oppression, first under Hitler 1939 to 1945, and later the Soviet Union until 1990. Could the West have prevented the Soviet takeover of Poland? Nobody cared to help them and the Allies did nothing, and the Cold War began. Once Poland fell into the Soviet sphere, the Allies branded them as an enemy communist state!

What an irony of the war games. In learning about subsequent historical information during the cold war, Poland's substantial contribution in WWII was consistently ignored or belittled. Until now, I see that what happened in WWII Poland still elicits uninformed facts and face-saving excuses. The Polish exiled army's slogan was.

'For your freedom and ours,' since they fought to liberate many countries from the Nazis. Ironically, they fought for the Allies to have freedom, and were left behind and forgotten.

Such brutal truth is avoided by the British on D-Day celebrations. Veteran Polish soldiers went to the Polish Club *(Polskie Ognisko)* at 55 Exhibition Road in Knightsbridge, London, disgusted at how they were betrayed. There was nothing for them to celebrate. There are probably very few or most probably none left by now!

My father just hung his head in despair about the absurdity of war and said.

"Life is an art. Living is an art. One has to learn how to live that art."

I am so grateful to him that he was not a victim of the Katyn Massacre, thus bringing me into the world to tell his story.

I can only guess he was philosophical enough about life to see it that way after all that he witnessed, experienced and ended up in exile. What else did he have after losing everything and arriving in England with nothing? Being positive and philosophical was a way to get through life as best as he could. Many Poles did not get through so easily and ended up totally crushed people, and some ended up mentally disturbed in hospitals.

My mama always lived with an anxious, suspicious, frightened and nervous disposition of fear if there were noises in the night, looking through the window to make sure she was safe.

Today, as an old man of 70 years of age, I am able to admire my parents' tenacity and strength to keep going no matter what they had to confront. There are millions of such war survivors not only from WWII but also from Korea, Vietnam, Cambodia and the many wars later and those currently being waged in North Africa.

I ask myself: What have we learnt and came to the conclusion that we have learnt "nothing" at all, except the continued advancement of a brutal world, with more advanced and better weapons to use against each other.

The reality about war and 'war crimes' came to me as I stepped into the shoes of my father and went on the journey with my father's war experiences in my mind, trying to recall the little that he told me. I tried to understand the gravity of the agony he endured.

I searched deeply into the dark hidden chasms of my soul and tried to find an explanation as to; "What is war and what are war crimes against humanity?" The explosive reality was too insane to even contemplate an answer, when the truth was blowing up in my face to the very core of my consciousness.

I suddenly entered an area that was formidable and frighteningly unpleasant to even wanting to know. I could not look away from the truth when it was presented to me. It was a dangerous truth, which was not comfortable to mention in our current climate of having to be politically correct, and attempt to challenge our democratic supressed right to freedom of speech.

War Crimes against humanity are punishable and those accused of such crimes are put on trial and either given a prison sentence or executed. I questioned how can there even be War Crimes against humanity, when "War itself" is a crime against humanity in the first place. Such a reality would become too dangerous to acknowledge, since many statesmen would become war criminals. How very paradoxical!

All I have left of my father from WWII are 'luckily' the following few photographs of him in his three different uniforms, along with a few photographs of my family, which were given to me by my parents many years before they died.

IN THE **POLISH** UNIFORM

My father, **Franciszek Faron**, at Polish Officers School in **1934** at age of 21 years: In the photo on the right, it shows that he was wearing "Puttees" instead of leather boots from the boot to the knee.

The Poles were too poor to manufacture full length leather boots like the Germans. 'Puttee" is a Hindu word for cloth wrapping, which the British military wore during their occupation of India in 'Colonial' times of the 19th Century into the 20th to World War 1.

IN THE **POLISH** COMBAT UNIFORM

Francizsek Faron in full Polish Combat Uniform **1939**
It is in this Polish uniform that he was later taken to Katyn, USSR, for execution and escaped from the train, making his way back to Silesia. The word "WOJAK" is written on the back of the photo, Which means "WARRIOR?"

THE TRIPLE SOLDIER And My Mother

IN NON-COMBAT **GERMAN** UNIFORM

On the left; my father in German army (Wehrmacht) uniform 1942. Given a new name of Franz Faron.

IN FULL COMBAT **GERMAN** UNIFORM

My Father in combat uniform after being forced into the German army
1942. Full German uniform for combat, including bayonets
He is the second from the right: Renamed to Franz Faron.

IN THE **BRITISH** UNIFORM

My father in FALKIRK, Scotland, **27th. May 1944** after being processed in the POW camp in North Africa and shipped to Scotland. He was preparing for the Invasion of Normandy in June 1944 under his new and assumed surname of **MICHOROWSKI**. It replaced his real name of FARON. This was arranged for him by the British.

IN THE **BRITISH** UNIFORM

1944: On the back of this photo is written: *"My most beloved Maria with love, Franek, 17/11/1944"*. He tried to send this photo to his wife from Holland, however, censorship disallowed it, since his identity would have been known in Poland.

IN THE **BRITISH** UNIFORM

1946: My father in 'British uniform' with the allied forces in 2nd Lieutenant Uniform. Renamed surname to Franciszek "MICHOROWSKI" in Osterbrock 1946. His name was later reinstated to his original name of **Franciszek Faron**.

NB: How rested and well fed my father looks in the 1946 photo.

CHAPTER TWO

My Mother 1920

Under the Polish flag:

Maria Malgorzata Superniok was born on 1st February 1920 in Brzezinka (German: Birkental), Upper Silesia, Poland. One of nine siblings; She was well versed in the languages of Polish, Silesian dialect, German, Czech and later spoke English very well.

My grandfather from my mother's side, Florian Superniok, was born: 24/11/1876 and died: 17/12/1951. *(I never met him).* He did take part in WW1 under the then Kaiser Wilhelm II, who was the last German Emperor (Kaiser) and King of Prussia, ruling the German Empire and the Kingdom of Prussia from 15th June 1888 to 9th November 1918.

The Kaiser was the eldest grandson of the British Queen Victoria and related to many monarchs and princes of Europe. Two notable contemporary relations being his first cousin King George V of the United Kingdom, founder of the House of Windsor, and his second cousin Tsar Nicholas II of the House of Romanov. The latter was the last ruler of the Russian Empire before the Russian Revolution of 1917 which deposed the monarchy. The area of Silesia came under the German Empire and Prussia, hence so many name changes of places in Silesia with the shifting borders.

According to my mama, her father was a wealthy man and the owner of a substantial estate with a hotel, bar and restaurant. The grounds had large linden and oak trees surrounding the hotel. There was a lake where people could go swimming during the summer months.

My mother grew up in wealth, privilege, received a good education, had servants and all the trappings that go with the upper classes. Her mother was from Vienna in Austria and also came from a wealthy family.

As I was growing up in London mama told me about the day her mother just dropped dead in front of her when she was only eleven years old. Her mother died of a massive heart attack and was gone in an instant. She was deeply grieved at her mother's funeral and was so devastated that she collapsed at the cemetery next to the grave. Maria missed her mother for many years to come. She was the youngest in her family and all her siblings were married and had left home.

My mother's father became a widower in 1931 and two years after his wife died he took a new wife in January 1933. My mother was almost thirteen years old when her father remarried and presented Maria to her new stepmother. From my mother's account, the disharmony and unhappiness at home with her stepmother began from the moment she met her. The hidden contempt for Maria was evident from the stepmother at first sight.

The stepmother wore long black dresses making her look austere and in control. She soon took over the household by sacking some of the household servants to save money. This woman disliked my mother intensely and made her life a misery, to the extent that she rationed her food and hid the bread away.

If Maria was hungry and caught eating more food in the kitchen the stepmother severely scolded her. Mama described her as a devious and cleverly deceitful woman, who got away with her cruelty beyond belief.

Her stepmother forced her to do all the housework, before and after school, making her feel like a poor Cinderella. The mental and physical cruelty went as far as beating her and locking her in the cellar. With that event my mother was outraged and retaliated furiously by fighting back. She refused to tolerate her stepmother's viciousness anymore, until her father stepped in and put an end to the abuse by this woman.

The years passed by in unhappiness for Maria as she was growing up and became a mature woman. However, my dear mama was destined for a very rough journey from thirteen years of age.

My mama (Maria) was already sixteen years of age when she met my father (Franus) on one Sunday morning at Holy Mass in the local church in Mikolow. Maria did not want to sit with her father because of her stepmother, so she chose to sit alone. Both Maria and Franus were in the same pew, with a few people between them and started glancing at each other, but too shy to speak with each other. As they left the church my father walked ahead of her and deliberately dropped his handkerchief in front of her. Maria picked up the handkerchief, walked briskly and called out to him, intuitively knowing that he did it on purpose.

"Excuse me mister. You dropped your handkerchief."

Looking at his blue eyes, fair hair and handsome face, she blushed and felt weak at the knees when he smiled so engagingly, with a very pleased expression of delight on his face. That was their introduction. Maria looked charmingly blushed with her peach coloured cheeks, coquettish smile, radiantly pretty face and Franus was enchanted to meet her. They both fell in love at first sight.

Maria was 16 years old at the time and fell in love from the moment she met with this handsome man, who was 23 years old. Their courtship was a long one and lasted for four years.

Her father was also a very strict man when it came to courtship regarding his daughter Maria. She was controlled with an iron fist by her father, as to when and where she could be with her fiancé. The years passed by and her only joy was having Franus in her life. By the age of 18 years of age Maria was able to access a modest allowance, which was left to her from her late mother's estate. That allowance gave her the freedom to seek an independent life away from her stepmother.

By late-1938 mama could no longer endure living under the same roof with her stepmother and courageously left home. Being from a prim and proper family in that period, leaving home for a single woman was difficult. Social attitudes towards a young unmarried woman living alone were very negative. It allowed for gossips to be perpetrated, with lies being spread through false suspicions of dangerous liaisons. However, she did not care and was strong enough to deal with things very well, with a fearless strength that put people in their place instantly.

Unfortunately, the relationship with her father became estranged since she left home and it became a painful period for her, especially when she needed help from her father, let alone from her stepmother, who remained unhelpful toward Maria.

She found a small bed-sit flat for herself in a nearby area called Podlesie, close to Mikolow. In the following year her father sold the estate in mid-1939 and moved to a small house in Mikolow. Mama never found out what happened to the estate after she left home.

Time passed and the story she was told by her only two surviving siblings, one brother and sister, was that the stepmother took the entire estate after my grandfather died. All was gone! The estate went into disrepair in the war and was finally abandoned.

I need to start with World War II and slowly build a picture of what I was told by my parents through my growing years. This will slowly unfold a story of my family just before I was born. So far it has begun with the year 1913 when my father was born. Let me now begin with the invasion of Poland as described by my mother.

Under the German flag:

It was only a short while ago when mama said goodbye to her fiancé at the train station in Mikolow, before he was sent to the war front to confront the German invasion. They embraced and held on to each other in desperation, knowing that it could be for the last time. The moment was disappearing quickly and the whistle blew for the train to depart. Franus squeezed Maria into himself and desperately passionately kissed her on the lips, which sealed their love forever.

Waving goodbye, with many others running along the platform with the train, Maria was crying with a bursting heart. Standing alone at the end of the platform, she wondered if she would ever see him again. As the advancing autumn wind gently caressed her hair she lost sight of him and the train, her soul was already feeling lonesome, lost without him. Maria stood still on the platform staring at an empty train track wondering what will happen to him.

She slowly turned away and began to make her way to the hat shop, where she was working as a milliner. Maria arrived at the shop in Gliwice drained of any feelings, sat down and pondered blankly for a while, temporarily motionless before picking up some fabric and started to make another hat for the shop. The ominous clouds of war were gathering on the horizon and the world would be changed forever.

On 1st September 1939 Poland was invaded by Nazi Germany. My mother lived in Podlesie near Mikolow, which was not far from the German border, and three days later the German soldiers came through the town. It was very early morning. The air was filled with the sound of marching soldiers on the cobblestoned streets vibrating through the ground, which echoed with a kind of permeating thudding sound in unison, waking the people of Mikolow.

My mother told me about that fateful day when the noise woke her up at 5 am. She got out of bed quickly and nervously looked through the window. The dawn was just breaking; her heart sank, trembling with fear in disbelief watching hundreds of German soldiers marching through the streets of town. As they passed by the soldiers banged on the doors of people's houses and ordered everyone out into the street to applaud the German army and raise their outstretched arms to Heil Hitler.

The hollow feeling of fear engulfing the human psyche, in the town, in the people and every fibre of her body was suddenly filled with the shock of the unknown at what was being witnessed. The invasion of Poland was taking place in front of her eyes and there was no stopping the onslaught of so much infantry marching in overpowering glory.

Maria felt so alone and could only think about the love of her life, Franus and where he might be trying to fight such a massive occupation of Poland. She knew he was ordered to meet the invasion head on at the border, when she said good bye to him at the train station.

She wondered what had happened to him if the German forces were marching through town in such triumph. Mama was feeling in a limbo of dread with not knowing what might have happened to him. All she could do was to pray for his safety and believe he was alive. In her mind she kept the last image of his face and kiss at the train station, which remained in her heart, giving her the strength she needed to face the invasion of Poland by Germany.

Mama did as she was ordered. Being afraid, she got dressed in a hurry and went outside along with everyone else in the house. Standing bewildered in the crowded street, she looked at the trees for a brief moment and noticed a hint of autumn showing. It was cool with an overcast sky, as a light breeze stroked her face and hair.

The air was filled with a nervous chaos of uncertainty and she felt an empty nauseous feeling in the pit of her stomach. She just stood there, with a blank look on her face. Wrapped in her woollen cardigan shivering, feeling isolated, alone, bewildered and lost. She was dumbfounded like everyone else. They all obeyed as they were ordered, or be arrested on the spot if resisting. Thousands of German soldiers marched through the town, which seemed to be like a long time.

All the people realized that the occupation by Germany was real. The trembling citizens of Poland were unprepared for the Nazi boot, even though the Polish army resisted heroically, the people obeyed orders rather than be shot. They obeyed without resistance, because being in a war zone, surviving was paramount to be there for your loved ones, which was all that mattered.

Mama's mind was filled with millions of scattered thoughts as to what would happen. Where was life going to take her and worst of all was suddenly having to face the unknown? These world events were going to change life as she knew it and also for Poland forever. The grim reality of what had taken place was actually unfolding in front of her.

Food was the most precious commodity to possess at a time like that. I remember her telling me of one incident in 1939, when the soldiers forced the people to throw out all their food into the street and to stack the butter into a separate pile. In her questioning mind she naturally thought that the German soldiers would take it all for themselves as supplies.

To my mother's horror, once all the food and butter were stacked in the street, the German soldiers were ordered to set fire to it with a flame thrower and moved on. Together with other people, she quickly grasped some utensils and tried to scoop up the melting butter running through the cobblestones' grooves and into the gutters. That was the only way of salvaging some butter for them. It was an unimaginable moment that was such a stressful memory and I watched her clasp her hands reliving the emotion.

Mama was fluent in speaking German as her mother spoke only German at home, since she was originally from Austria, but lived in Breslau (Wroclaw), Silesia. It was a great help for her when dealing with the German soldiers and throughout the war. With the invasion came the brutality and shock of war, suddenly witnessing all the death, depravation and suffering around her. Everyone was afraid of the future and what would happen to them.

It was a time where one had to be very careful of what you said and always remain vigilant about criticizing anything about Germany or The Third Reich; otherwise the consequences were too frightening to imagine. You either went to prison, or faced death by firing squad or were dispatched to Auschwitz.

The lack of food, lives lost and lives born, all taking place at once with no tangible reality of what the next day will bring for simple survival was an ordeal for everyone. Mama was a strong woman to keep going on in spite of the terrible surroundings she found herself in. Whatever circumstances were presented daily, mama had to play it well and keep a low profile to stay away from any conflict with soldiers and avoid arrest or death. This was a difficult time for her, since she had to survive alone without any help from her estranged father, in a time where death and destruction surrounded her everywhere.

Mama sometimes looked to nature for solace to find peace and tranquillity in silence and went for a walk through a small forest nearby. It was already cold and mid-autumn with a hint of winter to come. She was so aware of the silver birch golden leaves gracefully floating down around her. The gentle wind played with her hair as she was thinking of her Franus. She was with him in mind; dreaming of him wondering and hoping if he was somewhere safe. The winter passed by and soon it was going to be March followed by an early spring.

Maria kept working as a milliner at the small hat shop in Gliwice, which is a small town dating from the 13th century. The shop where she worked was still active from the early 1900s period. Her colleagues at work were the only sane contact with the outside world amid the chaos. The once tangible world she could relate to still existed inside the old walls of that shop. After finishing work one day she took the train to Mikolow and walked to catch the bus to go home.

It was getting dark, cold and damp with a slight drizzle falling. It was evening with a darkening sky and heavy greying clouds in March 1940. Franus just arrived in Mikolow from the Eastern front alone, dressed in what looked like old farmers clothes and looking totally haggard from the long trek back to Silesia from Russia. He went to Podlesie and was hiding behind some bushes, waiting nearby to see if Maria might be on the usual bus she used to come home on. He was so anxious to find her and felt as if he had been to hell and back. All he wanted was to be in her arms again.

The bus arrived. As Maria was getting off the bus in Podlesie, suddenly, out of nowhere like a miracle, she thought she could hear the love of her life calling from somewhere. Franus was calling out her name in a low voice and running to her. Recognizing his voice she turned around in disbelief totally surprised. She saw him and just embraced him in tears of joy holding on to him tightly. Franus was in bliss to be in her arms once more. He was unrecognisable with a beard, tired, emaciated, dirty and exhausted.

Keeping her voice low not to attract any attention, Maria stepped back to look at him properly and her heart sank on seeing Franus in such a dreadful state, yet overwhelmed to see him. She was saying.

"Franus, my loving Franus. I don't believe it. Thank god you're alive. My god! Franus what are you doing here?

"Maria, German soldiers are everywhere and we might be arrested if they find me." Franus said urgently.

"What on earth happened to you?" Maria asked.

"I'll tell you what happened later. I must hide" Franus said.

Maria instinctively sensed the sudden fear of being seen and arrested by the German Gestapo was terrifying. It was already dark and a soft drizzle was falling as two lovers were staring into each other's eyes.

Time stood still for a while at the bus stop. Maria was stunned and bewildered to see Franus again, as she looked at him with so much tenderness amid the circumstances that surrounded them. It was almost like an unconscious timeless situation of a trancelike dream of great happiness, impossible to understand amid the fear confronting them.

The gentle falling rain was settling on his face, hair and beard, as Maria was trying to comprehend his presence. She touched his cracked lips with her fingers and then looked into his soul through his eyes, wiping off the rain from his face. She held and looked at his hands and was deeply touched in her heart on seeing how rough and wounded they were, from the struggle to get back to her.

They quickly fled to Maria's flat in Podlesie. The one bed-sit flat was modest but elegantly furnished. There was a single bed, a small wardrobe, a small couch, kitchenette and a dining table for two. A small dressing table and mirror was in the far corner of the room next to a window, with elegant sheer lace curtains, letting a diffused light into the room. Her Persian carpet, beautiful porcelain crockery, china figurines, crystal vases and glasses were mostly from her mother's home. There was a small bathroom with toilet and bath tub near the bed. She was fastidious in keeping her flat spotlessly clean and tidy. Her bed was perfectly made up with beautiful linen.

Maria looked at Franus awkwardly and just said.

"Franus would you like to clean up? Here are some towels and that's the bathroom."

He went into the bathroom without saying a word. There was nothing for Franus to wear unless he reused the dirty clothes he arrived in. She got a clean sheet and a blanket out of her wardrobe to give to Franus when he finished washing. She handed him the sheet and blanket. Franus wrapped himself with the sheet and sat down on the couch looking like a Roman dressed in a toga. They were alone together in that flat for the very first time. Maria never had a man in her flat before.

Maria and Franus were a bit lost with this sudden unexpected situation presented to them. Maria felt awkward, as did Franus, being in such a very private feminine room. However, that was the catalyst to end their romance of an amazingly long engagement, which was in fact the beginning of their lives together.

The war did not mean anything to them in the moment, as if the noise of gun fire or bombs were not heard or even existed. They were overjoyed to be together again. Her prayers were answered. They could not take their eyes off each other, as their joy and happiness was overpowering. The next day she nervously went out to buy some male toiletries for Franus, plus clothes and pyjamas as he had nothing. That alone was difficult for her to do, as buying only male accessories looked suspicious under the circumstances.

Maria knew nothing of what he went through in Russia and escaping the Katyn Massacre until he told her the story. Maria was without words about Katyn, thankful he managed to avoid such a murderous end, and nursed him back to health.

Maria just stared into his eyes.

"Franus, Franus my darling. Thank god you're here with me. I missed you and love you so much. I prayed and prayed for your safety and now you're here." She smiled radiantly.

Franus looked at her beaming face and with a smile said.

"Maria darling I think we should get married as quickly as we can."

They quickly decided to get married in a hurry on 25th March 1940 at the local church in town. Mama quickly made her own wedding dress and veil in time and bought Franus a new suite for their wedding. All they managed was one wedding photo for their eventual future children. There was no party, reception or anything to celebrate. They were happy to have each other. They were finally husband and wife and became my parents.

They existed in a secret dream world, hiding in blissful happiness, as if the war never existed for them. Their created fantasy world was soon to come to an abrupt and unexpected end.

Not long after their marriage they were both arrested and taken to meet the Gestapo. They were driven to a beautiful large 18th Century house, which was occupied by the Germans and used as the local headquarters. After a lengthy interrogation, by a tall formidable and very confident, direct, intimidating Gestapo, Franus was renamed to 'Franz.' He was ordered to sign a paper to be accepted into forced labour. He was sent to collect his 'work-book' (Arbeitsbuch) and relocated on the spot. The heavily built imposing Gestapo stood up, leaned over his desk and said.

"Herrn Faron, you speak German very well with an educated manner, welcome to The Third Reich. Heil Hitler!"

The Gestapo then stood up and proudly outstretched his arm as my father left the room. Having no choice, my father signed that document and his life was changed in an instant. From that moment he was forced into labour for some German company. He was promptly sent to an unknown destination without any further consideration as to his Polish identity.

My mama just sat quietly in the Gestapo's office bewildered and speechless at what took place. She felt struck down in total defeat and motionless for a moment. The Gestapo simply stood there and said.

"Frau Faron, you're free to go home. Heil Hitler."

On seeing the Gestapo's outstretched arm to heil Hitler mama forced an indicated lifting of her arm half way in return, turned away and left the room. Once outside the room and in the corridor my father was waiting for her. With a paled face of fear she embraced him in tears holding on to him once more. She had to say goodbye to her beloved husband in a brief moment for the second time.

In a frantic moment, knowing that Maria was pregnant, Franus held her shoulders, trying to appear strong for his wife and in desperation, looking almost speechless, said.

"Maria, when you have our baby. If it's a boy name him Walter. If it's a girl name her Sofia. Don't worry I'll be fine. Take care of yourself. I love you."

With that last request he had to go. He turned around, walked away and was gone. He felt as if he was struck by a lightning bolt and totally stunned with what happened.

There was no time for them be together a little longer. He was told to go and she stood there watching him leave. What happened to her Polish officer? She became the wife of a prisoner of The Third Reich, who was sent into an unknown void. My mother felt like a piece of stone. It was all too crazy for her to believe such a sudden turn of events.

They parted in great sadness and never heard from each other or met for almost three years. The change of situation became bizarre. She was all alone again and their surreal existence was terminated with the stroke of a pen. In the meantime mama kept living alone through the war, taking each day as it came trying her best to survive, always with her beloved husband in mind. The war machine kept going forward with the German occupation of Poland.

The deep droning sound of the aircraft engines from the mighty airplanes, which flew high in the sky dropping hundreds of bombs. The mass blanket bombings by the enemy and allied forces created a panic with incredible fear. The power and deafening noise of exploding bombs, killing and maiming people, the devastation of houses being hit and the falling debris all around her. The flames, choking dust and smoke, people screaming for help.

The trembling shocked citizens of Poland were suddenly facing an Armageddon, unleashed indiscriminately on the innocent without any mercy, pity or anything that resembled some order in the chaos of the acrid smell of exploding gun powder. It was a terrifying hell that was unleashed in full force. Everyone was running in all directions traumatized screaming.

"Oh my god! Jesus Maria! Help me! My child! My child! Where is my child? Over here, over here, please help me, please help me!"

Blood was splattered everywhere. People were groaning, crying, trembling with hysteria and shock. The bombs were falling and a man in the street called out to my mama.

("Pani, Pani – tam - pod samochodem!") "Lady, Lady – over there, get under the truck."

She quickly ran to crawl under the truck and the man who helped to direct her was hit by an exploding bomb. He lay there in front of her groaning from pain. After the air raid was over she tried to help him. She was pushing his entrails back into his abdomen as he died watching her do it. Then she was helping other people, the wounded and maimed in the street, carrying the dead from the road.

The German soldiers simply ordered the people to pile up all the dead bodies and throw them into an open truck, when it passed through town. Where was there a moment to grieve and understand what had happened? Mama was trembling from shock and shaking like a leaf in the wind with her teeth chattering uncontrollably.

Mama was already heavily pregnant by this time in December 1940 and my father was away in a labour camp working for Germany. By late January 1941 she was in labour with birth pain and made her way alone to her flat in Podlesie. With the help of a midwife she gave birth to a son and named him Walter, as my father asked. Being all alone there were no celebrations, gifts or any kind of help and the only thing on her mind was how to survive with a new born baby. In her arms she nursed her baby with joy, as if she was holding part of her husband, wondering where he could be. The happiness of having their baby was lonely and challenging, not knowing how she will be able to manage with the circumstances that surrounded her. The months went by and the war continued relentlessly.

People were trying to hide in cellars to avoid the bombs, which was terrifying, as mama held on to Walter in her arms. In one incident they were hiding in a cellar with a few people and two German soldiers.

There were about ten people, men and women, including one woman holding her screaming new born baby and the two German soldiers. It was dark and dingy with only one light bulb burning. The pile of coal stacked in the cellar made it difficult to find a space to be still, as mama tried to settle upon the black coal and hold on to Walter.

The cramped conditions and fear was pervasive, that only silent waiting existed. They just starred at each other, which seemed like a dark vacancy of timelessness, listening for another bomb explosion. The baby kept screaming and the mother was anxiously trying to pacify her baby as best she could. Everyone was hoping it would calm down, because they could see that it was irritating the German soldiers.

One of the very irritated soldiers grabbed the screaming baby by its little hand and ripped it out of its mother's arms, hurled the baby against the brick wall, killing it instantly. Blood splattered on the wall and onto the mother's face and clothes. The woman went insane and started screaming hysterically from shock and kept on screaming uncontrollably, until the German soldier took out his pistol and shot her in the head.

A splash of blood landed on my mother's hair and dripped down her forehead. Mama was rigid, her heart thumping in panic and held on to Walter tightly, making sure she would not face the same fate. Everyone was silent shaking from fear, hoping they would not be the next victim of a bullet.

She was trembling, almost vomiting from witnessing such terror inflicted onto innocent people. Amid all this incomprehensible turmoil of fear and uncertainty mama was immobile and voiceless. It was no longer a normal world, but was instead emotionally charged through terror and the total insane circumstances of war.

I just listened with astonishment, trying to comprehend what my mother was telling me. She was reliving those unbelievable moments in tears. The grief so deeply plagued her in the future. She was exhausted remembering to tell her story to me and shaking. I really have no idea how she managed to remain sane after experiencing so much tyranny.

I had to console mama for a while, as she relived that moment with tears rolling down her cheeks with sweaty hands and forehead, trying to hold on to what she wanted to tell me. It was extremely difficult to retell such a harrowing memory, but she kept going on as if she had to tell me to unload her pain. I gave her all my compassion and empathy that I was able to. I am so grateful today that she had the strength to tell me so much.

My mother was indeed an incredibly very courageous and strong woman, for me to admire, that she survived such nightmares during the war. That is what the war was all about. Killing, raping, destroying and frightening everyone into submission. The dream of Hitler's 'Third Reich' was underway in full force and progressed relentlessly with a brutality beyond understanding.

The people were helpless and endured a hell unleashed on them that has never been and never will be forgotten. One day the Gestapo drove into the town square of Mikolow to address the local people, who were forced to gather and listen. The well-dressed SS Gestapo stood up in his open-hooded car and despotically delivered his speech to the people in German.

"You are either German and with us or you are Polish. If you are with us we will protect you and your children can join the Hitler Youth *(German: - Hitlerjugend)*, and the men will become part of the German army (Wehrmacht). If you choose to remain Polish and belong to Poland then you will not be treated as German."

My father originally being a Polish officer, my mother naturally chose to remain Polish and forfeit German privileges in defiance, after what happened to my father being forced into a German labour camp.

It was mid-winter with subzero temperatures, ice and snow cutting into the very bones of a person when one of mother's sisters, Gertrude, 17 years senior to her, died of Tuberculosis (TB) in 1941. Mama's father was very ill with pneumonia at the time and was confined to his bed, so he was unable to assist. Mama went to the hospital and asked for Getrude's body; she was told that the hospital morgue was full. The body of Gertrude *(my aunt)* was amid a pile of frozen corpses, which were stacked up at the back of the local hospital in Mikolow, as they ran out of space.

When mama went to find her sister's body, she was shocked in disbelief that Gertrude was at the bottom of a pile of dead bodies. Her older sister, my aunt Stefania, helped mama to find their dead sister's frozen body from under the pile of frozen corpses and give her a proper burial.

It was no longer a sane world, and the horrors that confronted everyone were insane. The altered state of this murderous world was beyond any reality or anything recognizable of life lived before the war, which was now gone, extinguished and no longer existed or was even reachable, under the new power of Nazi Germany.

As I listened to mama's experiences she would have quiet moments to catch her breath and memories. She would often appear to be deep in thought and almost rigid, staring into one place of the room. When I asked her where she was she suddenly woke up, as if from a trance, and said:

"I was thinking about the war and my father and all the difficult times I remember about him, that it sometimes steels my time away from forgetfulness. I wish I could be left with only happy memories. Ah! What dreadful times they were?"

Then she would shrug off the subject and get on with life. Through my empathetic nature, which has always stayed with me, I felt helpless to help mama and ended up just listening to her unload some of her pain. That is why I remember so much about the war and her sufferings. I am grateful today that she told me so much, whereas my father was far more reticent and rarely went into such detail talking about the war.

A FAMILY PICNIC, MIKOLOW **1908**

Silesia / Poland: 1908. **From left to right:** In the bottom part of the photo the three children (my two uncles and aunt) are the siblings of my mother well before she was born. The children on the right belong to the servants of the Superniok household. In the upper part, from the left, are my grandparents with their eldest daughter, Gertrude and some family friends.

MY MATERNAL ANCESTORS 1904

From left to right: Grandmother, Maria: born - **1881**
Grandfather, Florian: born - **1876**
Great grandmother, Apolonia: born - **1842**
Great grandmother, Marie: born - **1851**
Child in the middle (my Aunt), Gertrude: born - **1903**

In that period it was common practise to name ones children after their grandparents; As I was named after my paternal grandfather

THE TRIPLE SOLDIER And My Mother

My mother, Maria on her first birthday in **1921**.

My mother on her first Holy Communion in **1931**.

My maternal Grandfather **1915**.

My parents, **1936** during their courting days.

THE TRIPLE SOLDIER And My Mother

MY PARENTS' wedding, 25th March 1940 in the main 12th century church In Mikolow – Silesia/Poland
Maria Malgorzata Faron and Franciszek Faron

Maria Faron holding her son Walter,
December **1941.**

CHAPTER THREE

A Painful Journey

1942

Germany unleashed a terror, which in today's terms is more like a science fiction movie. On April 27, 1940, Heinrich Himmler ordered the construction of a new camp near Oswiecim, Poland (about 37 miles or 60 km west of Krakow). The Auschwitz Concentration Camp ("Auschwitz" is the German spelling for "Oswiecim") quickly became the largest Nazi concentration and death camp. By the time of its liberation, Auschwitz had grown to include three large camps and 45 sub-camps.

From here my mama's mental anguish and difficulties began, caring for her son without having her loving husband beside her. She lived not very far from Oswiecim/Auschwitz, *(which is a town where the concentration camp was located)*, about 30 kilometres (18 miles) from Mikolow. She knew that so many people were sent to that concentration camp and most of them never came out again. The horrors of Auschwitz were not fully understood in the world until the end of the war. However, the people in that area had an idea of what was going on in the camp. My mother had a Jewish school friend, Abram, who was arrested and sent to Auschwitz.

One morning mama decided to visit her best friend, Magda, who was taking care of her dying mother in Oswiecim. It was a depressing day with a grey overcast sky. As she passed by the concentration camp and looked at the slogan over the large entrance to the camp, which read: 'Arbeit Macht Frei' meaning; 'Work Makes (you) Free. She stared down the road at the gateway, like peering into a portal to hell with disbelief, thinking how was this possible to be happening and why. She was left with only a feeling of nausea and trembling fear in witnessing such a place at the gates of a world beyond imagination. My mother told me of the stench that was blowing in the wind from the burning bodies.

Compassion, help of any kind, resistance or a questioning of such injustice by going to any authority to stop what was taking place no longer existed. All that was left was her determination and strength to make sure that she did not end up in Auschwitz herself. Satan was now in charge, with a heartless ruthlessness beyond comprehension. The stench of death and suffering was overbearing.

She surprisingly saw her school friend, Abram, through the barbed wires and waved to him to come closer to the side, far away from the gate. He walked a bit closer to the wire fence looking stressed, anxious and afraid on his face. He stopped and just stared at Maria from a distance. She wondered why and threw him an apple over the fence, which she had in her handbag. Suddenly she felt the cold steel of a pistol pressed against her temple. Slowly turning her head to see who was holding the pistol to her head was an unthinkable surprise.

She recognised him and he slapped her on the face with anger. She was astonished that it was her childhood friend, Hans, who was also a mutual school friend of Abram. Hans was dressed in a German soldier's uniform and deliberately spoke only in German. He was confused and agitated; confronting his own split loyalty to the truth of his morality and humanness within his heart then sternly said.

"Maria, if you're ever found doing that again you'll also be sent there and join Abram. Do you understand? Now get out of here!"

With a stunned look on her face, her body trembling, she realized that keeping away was safer and Hans let her go. Mama just stood there looking at both of them in bewilderment and could not understand the terrible situation. Three school 'friends' were confronted with a surreal moment; each one being in a different reality simultaneously. It was impossible to believe that this situation had any sanity. What a paradox? The moment was mind blowing and she then slowly made her way to see Magda's mother.

So many frightening things were happening all around her, and she felt so very alone. Her siblings were not able to help her because they had their own difficulties under the circumstances. Even her father, especially her stepmother didn't want to help her. What would happen to her and her son?

A few months later she got word that Magda's mother passed away. Magda wanted her friend to be with her for the funeral in support. It was a sunny day in 1942. Mama left Walter with her sister and went to the funeral. The funeral was taking place in Magda's home town of Brzezinka/*(Birkental)*, where a sub-camp of Auschwitz was operational.

While she was there she never managed to see Magda or go to the funeral. Instead, on arrival in town everyone was ordered to stand in the street and watch prisoners being transported on foot from an Auschwitz sub camp passing through town.

They were ordered to walk all the way to harrowing forced labour. As she watched the weak and emaciated prisoners, in their striped pyjama like cloths walk through town, some of them were collapsing and dying on the way from hunger and exhaustion. They had blank faces without any expression, and once again everyone was ordered to throw all the dead into the truck that followed at the end of the march.

To my mother's disbelief, her friend Abram, whom she saw in Auschwitz, was among the dead. She was traumatised, voiceless and ill. My mother became numbed, crushed from within, her body shaking, feeling nauseous and shattered by the experience, as were all the living. The world she once knew had crumbled around her and disappeared with a helplessness that became nothing more than how to stay alive for the sake of her son and survive amid the surreal insanity she witnessed. After that mind bending soul stabbing torture she went home, unable to compose herself enough to attend the funeral. Almost half a century passed before she would meet Magda again.

AUSTRALIA 1990:

We were living in Australia when the Berlin Wall came down and Poland was finally freed from Russian occupation since 1945. I decided to take my mother to Poland. She was saddened that my father never lived long enough to see Poland free again.

During our visit to Poland we spent most of our time with our relatives, which were indeed very emotional, as you can well imagine after 45 years. Meeting family members for the first time was a very sentimental journey for me. Mama decided to find her dearest school friend, Magda in her hometown of Brzezinka *(Birkental)*, whom she had not seen since WWII in 1942. When we were in the town of Brzezinka mama remembered the little shop, which Magda used to own fifty years ago. She found the shop, which survived the war and was still there unchanged after all this time.

Mama stepped into the shop and stared at the old lady behind the counter, ready to ask her if she knew Magda. Before she could ask, mama was greeted with a gasping recognition by this old woman, who almost screamed in disbelief from her joy saying.

"Maria *(Marisa)*, my God, Maria *(Marisa)* I don't believe my eyes. Is that really you?"

Magda leaped from behind the shop counter with arms wide open to embrace her in bewilderment and joy that her dearest friend was still alive. Magda immediately closed the shop and took mama and me to her house.

My mother meeting with Magda in
Poland **1990** after almost 50 years.

As I watched Magda take mama under her arm it looked as if Magda was at least twenty years older than my mama and was looking more like her mother. It was so evident that the ravages of WWII had taken a huge toll on Magda, which was not over and still current with the living conditions under the Stalinist communist regime, imprisoning Poland since 1945. Finally the oppression was over in 1990 for not only Magda but also for all of Poland, since the Berlin Wall came down.

We arrived at Magda's house, which remained undamaged from all the bombings during the war. We entered the house and they sat down to talk, as if no time had ever passed. All the furniture was older than me and looked like a movie set in the 1930's. Mama said.

"My god Magda, nothing has changed inside your house, everything is still as it was before the war. I tried to see you in 1942 to attend your mother's funeral, but that wasn't possible because the prisoners from Auschwitz were marched through town that day and so I never got to see you."

"Yes I remember that awful day, Maria *(Marisa)* let's not talk about it and enjoy our time now." Magda said.

Magda started to make some tea and find some biscuits to be hospitable. Then my mama went to the sideboard to get some cups and cutlery, which was also where it had always been since she was a child playing with Magda there in that house. I was silent not wanting to interrupt their conversation and felt like I was watching and experiencing a real time warp, observing two old ladies who had gone to heaven for a while into their childhood.

I glanced at a photo of Magda's wedding and thought what a beautiful woman she once was. It seemed a strange situation of timelessness in such an amazing situation. They talked and talked for a long time until it was late and we had to leave. Arrangements were made to meet again but never eventuated, as Magda fell ill and could not see us before we left Poland. A few months after our return to Australia mama got word that Magda had passed away peacefully. It was sad news for my mother but at least she managed to see her one more time.

***

In Auschwitz alone the casualties of death was appalling. Not only Jews were in the camps but also millions of non-Jews died throughout all the camps in Europe. My mother was also terrified to be taken away and used in sexual slavery. In that time mass rapes were committed against Polish women and girls, followed by mass executions with shooting ethnic Polish women after the rapes were carried out.

Additionally, mass raids were reported, made by Nazi forces in Polish cities with the express aim of capturing young women, who were later forced to work in brothels attended by German soldiers and officers. Girls as young as 15 years old, who were ostensibly classified as 'suitable for agricultural work in Germany,' were also forced to work as prostitutes for German soldiers at their place destination.

These despicable atrocities were real and terrifying for young non-Jewish Polish women. I met one of those women who survived such brutality and eventually migrated to Australia. She was a wonderful person, who managed to overcome that entire trauma and live out her life happily and enjoy having her own family.

Strangely enough mama also told me that many German people around her were not all like the Nazis. They were as terrified as everyone else with what was taking place when the German army suddenly occupied Poland. They were as helpless as everyone else to stop what was happening and could do nothing about the situation.

In reality it is too often overlooked that approximately 5 million NON Jews also died in the holocaust throughout Europe. Unfortunately most films depicting the holocaust are usually dealing with the Jews and omitting the rest, giving a false impression of reality instead of the truth. Auschwitz/Oswiecim alone was a place where the Germans killed more than 100,000 NON-Jews: The Holocaust of the Jews was part of a larger German fantasy about a Master Race in control, which also called for the genocide of other undesirables, such as the entire Polish nation.

Poland became another useful dumping ground for millions of people from all over Europe alongside Austria, Belgium, Germany, Lithuania, Czechoslovakia, Estonia, Finland, Holland, Italy, Latvia, Russia and Yugoslavia to be accommodated in the Nazi Camps. My mother was aware of the events taking place around her. Eventually she had to make decisions as to where to go and what to do. She realized that even speaking fluent German would not save her.

She was deeply fearful and careful of accidently saying something politically incorrect, which could put her into Auschwitz, regardless of whether one was German or Polish. It made no difference as everyone was expendable. Her worst fear of all was what would happen to her son if she were killed.

AUSTRALIA 1994: Howling in the Desert:

We were already living in Australia since 1968. I took my mama to Uluru (Ayres Rock) in the Northern Territory by car. I was 48 years old by then and mama asked me to take her to see the Australian desert. I was alone with my mother driving for three days through the desert until we reached Uluru, which lies in central Australia.

As we arrived at Uluru, the largest rock in the world, and the Olgas, we were truly amazed with the unforgettable sight, which we beheld and experienced in our souls. We were among a crowd of onlookers watching Uluru and the Olgas in the setting sun. The changing colours of the desert at sunset is to be experienced in the flesh, which was evident, as the cameras of the present tourists were hard at work to capture the moments of change. It is a unique sight to behold and I am so glad my mama was able to be there sharing it with me. Those moments of splendour in the desert will stay alive in my memory for as long as I live.

The sun was sinking behind the horizon rather quickly and I asked mama if she would like to drive out at night, a small distance to be away from any hotel lights. I wanted her to observe and experience the night sky in total darkness. She was delighted with my suggestion and off we went to star gaze.

When the desert sky at night is uninterrupted by any city or man-made lights, it appears as if you could almost touch the stars. The air at night is crispy cold and so crystal clear in the desert that the Milky Way becomes a breathtaking awesome sight, like looking at jewels in the night sky. I decided to lie on the sand, still warm from the day's heat and look at the stars. I asked my mama to do the same.

As I sank my fingers into the soft warm sand I was left speechless, looking into god's window of eternity. My body seemed to melt into the blood red desert sand around me and unite me with the universe above, with a feeling of total oneness. There are no words to be spoken, as only the soul is able to feel for which there is no language. We lay there in silence side by side and allowed the universe to speak into the soul. Tears ran down my cheeks, with the knowledge of being a particle of the universe that engulfed me.

In a transfixed moment I saw a shooting star streaking through the void, passing by our planet in a second and I felt as if the firmament spoke through my soul. It reminded me within the core of my consciousness about the living, the dead and the unborn. That you and I, the chance progeny of earth and time, dared to climb where we were born to grope and hideously rot. It was within this space of celestial existence, to be no more than that shooting star passing through space and time, and be gone from here in a cosmic moment, is what numbed me. It was a profound awakening of life's reality searching for itself in the present.

For me it was like being in a trance of nothingness, where ones ego is disarmed and laid to rest. Any importance you think you may have seems so futile and ridiculous in the face of all that is staring into your soul, while you stare back into it. Time is non-existent and the 'past' looks at you, as it once was millions of years ago.

The billions of stars, countless millions of light years away that is visible, and may no longer exist anymore, yet I could still see them. The past, the present and the future all existed at once and my consciousness remained suspended in the now. I was one with the universe for a fleeting moment in the cosmos. My body and mind were in a trance of silent stillness. I was alone, but joined with the night sky and the earth beneath me.

I then heard mama sobbing from the intensity of a wakening soul under heaven. Memories that haunted her from the past still held her captive from the war. I sat up and talked with her to console her. I could see tears rolling down her cheeks in the dim light of the brilliant Milky Way glowing in the darkness.

I asked mama why she was crying. She was unable to speak and was swept away into the deep chasm of the past, of all that she suffered in the war. The universe spoke through her heart and purged her soul for the first time after 47 years of bottled up pain and an unforgettable tortured mind.

Mama simply broke down howling and howling into the empty void of the desert sands and the stars above. I just sat there and let her cries and screams rise into heaven. Her howling was much overdue and this time the universe heard her pain, as well as the vast desert sands surrounding her. She was alone with me and held on to my hands, screaming out to be heard by god himself. In the end I nursed her in my arms like I would a child and said:

"Cry mama, cry and cry as much as you need to cry. I'm here with you and for you. Let the pain go. There is no need for you to suffer anymore. Mama, the war is over! It all happened a very long time ago."

MARIA AT AYRES ROCK (ULURU) AUSTRALIA **1994**.

I wept with her until she calmed down enough for me to take her to the car and drive.

I felt as if she finally needed to tell me her untold story so I took her back to the hotel. On arrival in the room the desert silence was powerful and in such profound stillness one could hear one's heartbeat. I made her a cup of tea and was poised for what she was about to tell me. It

AT ULURU WITH MY MOTHER **1994**.

was a very long night as she finished the story at dawn. Mama began to relate the entire journey she endured during the war.

Watching her tears slowly creeping down her cheeks, I quietly listened attentively to the whole ordeal that she experienced during the war. Like dark shadows of pain from the distant past in the war, mama was again reliving those moments. After my mother told me the whole story I was stunned, and wondered how she ever managed to survive the war. I took many notes at the time and will narrate, as best as I can, what my mother told me as follows:

In August 1942 mama received a letter from her husband, which she nervously read and wondered why it was written in German, signed, *'From your loving Franz.'* "Why was it not written in Polish?" She thought. He wanted to let her know that he was conscripted into the German army on 25th July 1942, in Breslau/Wroclaw, while working in the forced labour camp. At that time the Polish language was forbidden to be spoken in Breslau/Wroclaw and was punishable with beatings or arrest. Therefore he was forced to use his new German name of Franz, as all letters were censored.

Being stunned with this crushing news she was shaking and devoid of any emotion for a while and wondered what happened to Poland and her army. Was Poland now totally disintegrated with no army left? Her handsome Polish officer no longer existed and she had become the wife of a German soldier.

She felt betrayed and saddened, but most of all, was the fear that her husband was returning to the war front again. Mama wanted to go and see her husband in Breslau with Walter, in fear that he might die without ever seeing his son. However, it was not possible to take Walter or even try to go alone. She found out that he had already left Poland and was sent to the west by the time she received his letter. Mama was heartbroken for her husband.

The difficulty of obtaining food during the war was a very arduous process indeed. Mama was not eating enough food and suffering from malnutrition along with many others. As a result, she was suffering from tuberculosis. The incidence of tuberculosis, being a highly infectious disease, was rampant. Treatment for a cure was limited, involving a long time to get it under control and arrest the infection. She was already diagnosed and suffering with Tuberculosis (TB) at that stage.

Mama became critically ill and knowing the seriousness of her plight with TB, she was in a desperate situation as to how to take care of Walter. There was nobody to take care of Walter while she went to a Sanatorium in Bielsko Biala, approximately sixty kilometres away. In that time TB was very difficult to treat and highly contagious. Many people compared it to the bubonic plague and were very afraid of being near to anyone who had it. There was no other way for her except to place Walter into a convent.

By the autumn of 1942 mama placed Walter into a convent at Raciborz, Poland (Silesia). On arrival at the convent with Walter mama rang the heavy iron bell of the large wrought iron gates of the mighty building. The autumn golden leaves of the silver birch trees at the gate were drifting down around her as she waited at the gate.

A nun came to meet her, dressed in a long black dress and a covered head with a white starched wide brimmed hat. She opened the huge gate and asked mama to follow her to meet the mother superior. The convent was warm in the already cool autumn air outside.

She made her way up the grand staircase to mother superior's office. She received mama and Walter with kindness and told her to sit in a chair opposite her. Mama noticed a large painting of the Blessed Virgin Mary hanging on a distant wall, with a red candle glowing underneath the picture, and looked through the window at the Pidgeon's purring on the window ledge outside. She was anxious and very nervous with many distracted scattered thoughts. After mother superior interviewed mama she accepted to take Walter while mama went to the Sanatorium. She was so grateful, but at the same time torn apart, having to leave Walter behind in the convent.

Mama managed to visit Walter fairly regularly during her treatment and convalescence, for the first three months. She was not allowed to be near her son because of the TB. She was allowed to see him only through a glass partition. This isolation proved to be cruel and traumatic for Walter, not being able to be with his mother physically. When mama went to visit Walter, he screamed and screamed to be comforted by her when he saw her through the window.

Mama watched him as he tried to get away from the nun holding on to him. Then he was pushing the nun to leave him alone to get away from her and climbing up to the window ledge and banging on the glass screaming incessantly.

His tortured face and desperate look of appeal to the nun to allow him to get closer to his mother was denied each time she would visit him.

"Mama!"

He would scream over and over again, looking hot and red in the face from severe stress and crying, gasping to breathe to the point that mama could no longer endure such heartache anymore. She was beside herself with watching this unliveable situation she was trapped in, not being able to hold him. She would hear his screaming cries and just end up crying with him.

"Mama, mamaaa, mamaaa, mama." He was choking from lack of air.

It looked as if he was having huge and uncontrollable tantrums being separated from his mother. He was utterly stressed, hot and sweaty, ready to pass out and beyond control.

As she was leaving and walking down the long corridor of the convent, the echoing of his screams resonated in her ears, until his voice broke into silence and he could no longer scream, which was intolerable to bear. Mama was emotionally agonised to the point of also being traumatized. She left some new clothes for Walter and returned to the Sanatorium totally shattered, exhausted and drained of tears each time she visited him.

After three months she was forbidden to see Walter again because of, not only her fully active TB, but also the terrible emotional damage affecting both of them. She was kept in the Sanatorium for a further twelve months. Her health was deteriorating relentlessly. She gazed through the widow and watched the snow falling as winter approached and she drifted into her mind, feeling her son's pain of isolation in the convent and longing to be with him. Her melancholia about the separation from her son was taking a heavy toll on her health and emotional welfare.

Her condition deteriorated so badly that the doctors had to collapse the right lung to save her, because it was rotting away with the TB. Being separated from Walter was bad enough to bear, but to have to face losing one lung was like being a caged wingless bird in the existence of a human body, trapped into the confines of the Sanatorium and surroundings with nowhere to fly. After the lung was collapsed she slowly recovered. She lived in the Sanatorium, daily reading books or walking in the surrounding gardens, wondering if she would live or die.

She knew that the constant separation from Walter would end up having a negative effect on Walter's memory of his mother, if the nuns were the only substitute. Mama looked to nature again to find respite from the reality of her impending fears of losing Walter to the nuns. Her solitude in the innocence and harmony of nature became habitual.

The snow kept falling relentlessly and she was mesmerized by the silence. The snow was covering the ground and trees making the scene outside quiet, serene, still, pure white and clean. The deep green spruce trees were laden with snow and mama found nature's beauty consoling her soul for a while. She was yearning for spring, hoping it might bring her some happiness. It was already 1943 and time was passing without her husband and son.

Spring arrived and was quickly followed by summer. During the warm months mama was consoled by the purity of nature, and often walked into the lush green forests and fields, which were intertwined with the forests. The forest surrounded the Sanatorium giving the place a wonderful and tranquil serenity to convalesce.

Sitting on a log she would listen to the skylarks' chirping high in the sky. Mama looked at the green trees against the deep blue sky above and longed to get well enough to see her son and husband again.

She would contemplate about her years before the war and remember life then and all the happiness shared with her husband, how the world once was and at peace. She loved looking at the wild flowers, the squirrels and hawks and other wild life and feeling their freedom of life, which was denied to her and Poland. The sounds of silence and only bird songs, without hearing any gunfire or bombs, were cherished moments for her to feel at peace for a short moment in the quiet bosom of nature around her.

The year soon went into September again and another autumn arrived, when she went mushroom picking in the pine forest near the Sanatorium, as she used to do with her husband, to forget the pain of her lifeless existence. So much time passed by in the Sanatorium for mama during 1943 and she managed to get well enough to leave the Sanatorium for a short period and be united with her son again.

She went to the convent and finally brought Walter home with her for a while. On seeing Walter after eleven months she was amazed how much he had grown up and no longer cried when he saw her. He just looked at her blankly, as if he had forgotten who she was. Mama was shocked and deeply saddened with his expressionless face. For Walter she was just another trusting woman who came to take him away from the convent. Walter held her hand and he went home with her after being told that she was his mother.

It would have been late September 1943 and mama sat quietly at her home in Podlesie with Walter for a few days. She was so happy to have some precious time with her son after all those months without him. Walter was about two years and eight months old by then. It was a beautiful sunny day and mama decided to get dressed and go out with Walter for a walk. Then someone was knocking on her front door and she was feeling alerted, as she was not expecting anyone to visit, and went to open the door. She got the biggest surprise that she never dreamed of.

Her beloved Franus stood there with a big smile in a German uniform. She screamed, exploding with tears of joy. Seeing her Polish Officer as a German soldier hollowed her heart, which she chose to ignore.

"Franus, Franus my god it's you. I can't believe my eyes."

She threw her arms around him. She could not remember the last time she shed tears of happiness. It was so exhilarating to be with her husband again that all her pain evaporated into forgetfulness and replaced with heaven.

He so unexpectedly turned up on leave from the west for a very short furlough to visit mama and his son. My father saw Maria's sallow and emaciated face from the TB, which tore at his heart strings with concern, not knowing why she looked so sick.

"My god Maria what's happened to you? You look pale and unwell. Are you alright?" He said, holding her in his arms. She avoided the question looking lovingly at him and said.

"Franus come and meet your son Walter."

Walter was hiding behind his mother, holding on to her dress and staring at his father for the first time, who was dressed in a German soldier's uniform. He had never seen a man like that before. My parents noticed how shy and reserved Walter was, wary of meeting a stranger.

My father's reaction at meeting Walter for the first time was utter joy and jubilation, with his loving heart to see his son. He was overwhelmed, hugged and kissed him, being so proud to have such a handsome son. He was elated to not only see his son but also to be with his wife. Walter was quiet and subdued being with a stranger, who was so loving and attentive to him. Walter appeared lost and bewildered with this man, who told him that he was his father. Such a young boy was unable to understand the situation he was confronted with, as all he knew and remembered was the nuns at the convent. The memory of his mother was confused, faded and almost gone. This was a heartbreaking moment for my parents.

Mama was so happy and looked at Franus and said.

"My darling, I didn't want to tell you that I have TB. Please don't be afraid and I'm slowly getting better. I'll be fine and I'm continuously getting treatment. That is why I was allowed to have some time with Walter away from the Santorum."

My father was deeply troubled about my mother's illness, but they wanted to enjoy what little time he had. He was given only three days to see them before being relocated from Holland to northern Italy. What joy and happiness arrived for the three of them? It was like a blessing from god. My father was overjoyed and delighted seeing his wife and meeting his son for the first time.

Their reunion of joy and happiness was beyond words and was more like a brief encounter that almost seemed like a dream of great happiness that never happened. My father changed into civilian clothes, as he wanted a photo with his family but without his German uniform. He had one photo taken of them all together and carried it with him throughout the rest of the war.

Soon mama had to say goodbye to her Franus yet again and he promised her that he would return after the war was over. They stood in silence unable to speak; stared at each other and embraced with loving arms knowing that they may never see each other again. In deep consciousness of the reality of what his departure to the western front in northern Italy meant, was emotionally too terrible to contemplate.

My father hugged Walter tightly for a while as tears slowly began to trickle down mama's cheeks, trembling like an autumn leaf in the wind, holding on to my father's hands clutching each other, as their united hearts were both being ripped apart. Mama kept fixed on her husband's eyes, as he could no longer hide his tears for the first time. Their parting tears of great sadness were chokingly wordless and suspended in silence as he turned to leave and said goodbye. The utter emptiness of that parting moment is too tortuous to imagine. I am lost for words to express how this difficult painful parting would have been for my parents.

After my father left, mama sobbed her heart out. Soon she had to leave Walter at the convent again for a while until she finished her treatment at the Sanatorium for the TB. Being forced to stay away from her son was an agony that only a mother could understand. Mama's heart was shredded over and over by not being able to see Walter, caress and console him lovingly and hold him in her arms. It was a dreadful time.

THE TRIPLE SOLDIER And My Mother

POLAND 1943

Walter with both parents, only once, in Poland / Silesia, while my father was on furlough from the German army September **1943**. He was in civilian clothes, not wanting to be in a German uniform. My mother lost Walter a year later, whereabouts unknown. The inscription on the photo reads as: *(W Dowod wiecznego Pszywiazania mazyska)*
Translated: "In token of everlasting union in marriage."

This is the photo that my father carried with him throughout the war, when he promised my mother that he would come back to find her. That is why it is so damaged.

Many months passed by with intermittent visits with Walter during her healing period of convalescence at the Sanatorium. The chaos of the retreating German army around September/October 1944, as the Russians were advancing, created a great deal of fear for everyone. Mama became highly charged with anxiety about Walter's safety that she fled from the Sanatorium, without permission, still weak and ill from the TB.

She went to the convent and took Walter away with her to the one room bed-sit home in Podlesie, which was still there, empty and unoccupied. She was lucky enough to be able to keep that place for herself throughout the war. In fact the whole building was almost empty as so many people fled from their homes in fear of the bombings and destruction, as well as the advancing Russian army.

Mama lived there all alone in seclusion with Walter in that room for three months. During that time all the aggressive bombing and shelling between Germany and Russia was taking place, since that area was the War Front. Living in that area was a test of nerves and will power for everyone, trying to endure the murderous situation of so much fighting surrounding them. Many people were leaving and only mama's direct neighbours were left in the house that always took care of her flat while she was away.

In that confusion and danger mama took Walter and courageously attempted to cross the War Front three times in one night, with the help of a German army Block leader. On the third attempt she finally made it to her father's house, which was about four kilometres away. When she arrived with her son at her father's house mama begged, pleaded and implored her father to allow her to stay with Walter at his house. She was so very afraid of living alone in her flat in Podlesie, while the rest of the house was almost empty. Mama's stepmother refused to help her being afraid of the TB and her father quietly submitted and agreed with his wife.

Mama was totally devastated with the ruthless outcome and was helpless beyond feeling anything. Her father felt guilty and gave her a three-quarter length fur coat and told her to flee Poland and go to Germany before the Russians take over. She was stunned, speechless and desperate, as she cautiously made her way back to Podlesie again with her son.

Totally forlorn, lost and feeling abandoned mama sat there in her room, staring at her son sleeping peacefully not knowing what to do or who to turn to, as the night turned into day. On that morning in late December the postman came with a telegram. She wondered who could be sending her a telegram when she is all alone, not expecting anything from anyone.

As she opened the small envelope and read the short message inside, informing her that her husband was 'missing in action' since November/December 1943 in Italy, was like an intolerable stab in the gut. She fell to her knees distraught, as Walter silently watched in confusion and she plunged into a mental collapse with a scream in her heart.

"No! No! No! Oh god no!" She started sobbing uncontrollably.

When mama read the telegram, her entire world crumbled around her. She felt frozen in the moment of place and time, unable to move, hollow and empty of any feelings with a strange shock of disbelief, an almost unacceptable denial and lost in a numb oblivion. She was crushed into a shaking mental confusion, terrified that he was probably dead and her mind went into a whirling spinning vortex of convulsions.

In the end she was unable to cry from shock, staring into space where there was no space, just one room and her son. All she could think of was that Franus promised her he would return after the war was over.

Trembling with fear and shock she was left with only a flicker of hope, that somehow, somewhere her husband might be alive. Mama deeply believed in the power of prayer to the Mother of God; Our Lady of Czestochowa, who is the symbolic 'Queen of Poland.' Holding her rosary beads mama prayed and prayed. She wanted to believe he survived and that one day she would see him again. That belief gave her the strength of hope.

In her desperate confusion, surrounded by the insanity of war, she took Walter and fled from Podlesie together with a friend of hers,

Marta and her two little children, in fear of the Russian aggression and went to Germany. It was already December and the full brunt of an icy winter was ready to strike again.

They managed to find some transport, a truck to take them to Bad Landek *(Lądek-Zdrój in Polish)*, which is a small town in Lower Silesia, south-western Poland, and was still in Germany at that time. Using different modes of transport, as well as going on foot, it took them two weeks to get there. All she had with her were her identity papers and some other documents. She held her son in her arms and started to run to catch the transport.

Suddenly an exploding grenade blew up the water mains in front of her. Luckily they were unharmed, except for a surge of water covering her legs knee high. She was wearing felt boots that became totally soaked and froze almost instantly in a temperature below minus 20 degrees Celsius / (-4 Fahrenheit).

The intense cold was freezing her boots quickly and she simply had no time to dry them, except to get onto that truck and go. She held Walter and climbed aboard. She travelled in the damp cold boots for two weeks until they arrived in Bad Landek in late-1944. She found a school that was converted into a refugee shelter for thousands of people from all over Europe. Finally she had some shelter where she could take off her cold wet boots to dry and wrapped her legs in rags.

The refugee shelter was packed with people all trying to have a rest from the chaos and destruction they fled from. It was a place of total chaos, suffering, hunger, trauma and desperate lost people from many surrounding countries. They had nothing left except what they had with them in a suitcase and the clothes they had on themselves. It was a crying and grieving time for all those lost souls, who had nowhere to go. My mama was part of that lost world and the only thing left for her was to pray for her missing husband's safe return.

Keeping sanitation and using a toilet in such overcrowded conditions was another massive hardship beyond imagination. The frustrated, injured, desperate and mentally shocked were looking like wild people, some of whom had given up and were just like people without any expression or life left in them. Everyone was trying to keep their human dignity if possible. Others who no longer cared and simply stole whatever they had to, to stay alive. Only the strong willed ones were the ones who would make it to the bitter end of the war.

All this time Walter was kept warm with the fur coat that her father gave her. A new year began and Walter would turn four years old in January 1945 and mama's birthday was to follow soon after.

On the eve of her son's birthday she occupied the top bunk-bed in the refugee shelter. All the bunks were made from wood and were interconnected with each other. As she moved her body close to Walter, to hold and keep him safe in her arms, she tried to get some rest and settle to sleep. She finally closed her eyes and Walter was already asleep.

She was then woken by a strange sound of wood cracking followed with a movement of the bunks slowly leaning, as if they were gradually sliding in one direction. Then suddenly the loud noise of breaking wood was terrifying, as the entire row of bunks began to crash to the floor, with everyone screaming and screaming from the shock.

They were laying in the middle part of the long connected bunks and the whole row fell to the ground. Walter was free of injury but mama's body was punctured with nails and splintered wood in her back, legs and face. The scars remained throughout her life. She lay there bleeding and helpless and passed out from the excruciating pain and shock remembering nothing after that.

When mama regained consciousness, feeling pain and difficulty to breath, she found herself in a hospital bed severely wounded, also with a high fever from the TB. She gradually began to wake up, thinking and seeing more clearly but could not feel Walter's little fingers holding her hand. Not being able to find him mama suddenly panicked! She wanted to see her son. She could not see him and screamed.

"Where is Walter? Oh my God! Where is my son?"

The nurse came to see her and said.

"Maria, you arrived at the hospital alone twelve hours ago and unconscious. I'm sorry. Do you know anyone who might have looked after him?" We have no idea what happened to him."

Feeling delirious from her illness she could not think clearly and could only think that maybe Walter was lost or taken! In that moment all she wanted to do was to get up and look for her son. She found herself in too much pain from the injury and was calmed down by the nurses and doctor.

Mama found out later from other nurses that her friend Marta looked after Walter for a while until he got sick somewhere across the border in Czechoslovakia. She was bewildered to find out that he was taken to Czechoslovakia wondering how that could be possible. Why Czechoslovakia? Mama was in a state of grieving madness about the loss of her son and a husband 'missing in action.' She thought she was going crazy.

Unfortunately she did not know where Walter was. Having learnt that Walter might be in Czechoslovakia, the next night she defiantly ran away from the hospital in Bad Landek with her wounds unhealed. She was drifting through the streets in the area for one week, wondering aimlessly looking for Walter. In her desperation, every boy she saw she thought it was Walter. When she saw a little boy in the street she would run up to the child thinking it might be Walter. The reality of not finding Walter caused a permanently anguished grieving heart, but she could not give up her search.

In desperation she went across the border to Czechoslovakia and kept asking people in the streets if they saw a little boy looking for his mother. She was told by some people that perhaps he was in an orphanage in Ceske Budejovice, because there were a few Borromeo Orphanages in that city, which were run by the sisters of Charity. It was 150 kilometres south of Prague in Bohemia and about 360 kilometres from Bad Landek.

A nurse from the hospital took pity on my mother and rescued her from aimlessly roaming the streets to find Walter. That nurse willingly went on a quest together with mama to Czechoslovakia by train in search of Walter. It was so cold and mama started coughing so much from the TB. By the time she reached Ceske Budejovice she collapsed with blood gushing out of her mouth from her lungs due to the TB.

I will never understand how my mother managed to travel the

distance of 360 kilometres in search of her son. When I take into account of how very weak she was, it amazes me that she could survive. Her determination to find her son was relentless. She became obsessed to the point of suffering from some kind of mental fixation and stubbornness believing she would find him. Needless to say, she never did find him and eventually collapsed.

The nurse took her to hospital and mama ended up in that hospital for six months, receiving Pneumothorax treatment (injected air into the lung).

She was treated by a German doctor, Dr Berger, who was so very kind to her and most compassionately sympathetic to her situation. She never forgot the doctor's gentle smile and amazing loving goodness emanating from his heart and eyes. He was such a humane doctor, with genuine loving care, who was helping everyone from any country as much as he could. He turned out to be a truly wonderful doctor and a gentleman, who saved her life under such very difficult circumstances in the war.

During her six months in that hospital she contracted typhoid, paralysis of the legs and an infection of her left lung simultaneously. She thought she was going out of her mind crying inside nonstop. The nurse friend and Doctor Berger cared for mama throughout her sickness, which she managed to miraculously survive. However, mama always questioned herself, why could she not remember the name of that nurse, who gave her such amazing kindness. She could only remember her kind face, which remained a total mystery to her for the rest of her life. Who was she? Throughout her life mama truly believed that the nurse must have been an angel.

She had hardly been with Walter since he was 18 months old. By this stage mama finally lost faith in god or anything to give her hope. In her mind she was now screaming through her soul to god and the Virgin Mary. Blaming them for the betrayal and agonizing pain of losing everything she ever loved and was taken away from her. Why? Why? She questioned god angrily. She bitterly regretted that she ever left Podlesia in the first place. If she had stayed in Poland she would never have lost her son and perhaps would have recovered from TB.

She weighed only 43 kilos and was very emaciated from all the sickness. Yet she somehow miraculously recovered and survived the hospital in Ceske Budejovice, with the help of that wonderful doctor and nurse. **On 8th May 1945 the war in Europe was over.** Mama had nowhere to go so she left that place and made her way back to Poland. She was too tired and beaten to keep looking for Walter. She returned to her bed sit flat in Podlesie, which was still there in June of 1945, but Poland, along with Eastern Europe, was under the new ideology with Stalin's totalitarianism of Russian communism.

It was summer, sunny blue skies and warm, with green fields of different vegetables, golden fields of wheat and rye, swaying in the wind like waves on the sea. By now her TB was finally under control. She went for a walk in the nearby forest to regain a more positive perspective view on life from the silence in nature. Her mind was always thinking of her son and of her beloved husband. They were the only reason that gave her the strength to keep on living, in the hope they would one day be reunited.

She tried to adjust to some kind of routine again and went to Gliwice to see if the hat shop was still there and ask for work again. The shop owner was still alive and threw her arms around Maria with joy on seeing her and welcomed her back to work for her as before.

By then Poland was overrun by Russian soldiers, which created another world from what Poland once was. The German soldiers had retreated to Germany. Life was suddenly very different again under communist Stalinism. A new foreign power occupied and ruled Poland for the next 45 years.

My mother shook her head in dismay, struggling with the painful memories, as she looked into my eyes with tears again and attempted to continue. After a break she took a deep breath, dried her eyes and plodded on, only because I asked her to tell me more.

Mama tried to adjust to the new regime and system of fear under Stalin. One morning she put on her rouge velure hat and brown woollen coat as it was a cool, wet and windy day. She made her way to catch the bus to the train station in Mikolow to go to Gliwice.

As she boarded the train, she went into a compartment where

another lady was already sitting. Suddenly two Russian soldiers entered the same carriage. The lady got up and hastily left to go to another compartment as she must have felt intimidated and uncomfortable. One soldier was blond haired with pale skin and blue eyes and the other one was a Mongolian Russian soldier with black hair and dark brown eyes. Mama sat there alone with the two soldiers feeling uneasy and uncomfortable, as the train slowly pulled away from the platform.

Mama also decided to leave that compartment and find another one. As she got up to leave, the blond haired soldier blocked the door and pinned her against the door until she was unable to move or push him away. She couldn't breathe from fear with what was taking place. He stared into her eyes and moved forcefully close to her, squashing his body against hers. His lips were almost on hers. She was choking, trying to get away.

Turning her head to the side to avoid his mouth and lips; she panicked! Afraid, disgusted and repulsed; in desperation she began to say.

"Let me go. Please let me go. Get off me! Leave me alone."

He grabbed her throat and then fondled her breasts and thighs. Her hat fell off. She was petrified, struggling and trying to push him away, but he was too strong for her to move.

The train was travelling at full speed by then and she could not get away from him. Once she realised what he was going to do to her, mama screamed out for someone to help her. In that instance the Mongolian soldier was there watching and grabbed the soldier's coat from behind, pulled him away and threw him against the compartment window yelling.

"Leave that woman alone!"

She was so relieved and thankful to that Mongolian Russian soldier and just looked at him with so much gratitude for helping her. She was amazed how human goodness is able to shine through, even in such a dreadful situation. Her hair was dishevelled and her hat was on the floor. Her dress was slightly torn at the top. She was trembling from the attack. She picked up her rouge coloured velure hat and left the carriage.

When she arrived at the hat shop in Gliwice she was shattered, shaking like a leaf and broke down falling into a chair exploding into tears, sobbing in despair from such a personal violation of her personal space on the train.

The three women in the shop realized the seriousness of her breakdown and dropped everything rallying to her side, hugging Maria asking her what happened. She was sobbing uncontrollably, feeling so downtrodden and unable to speak. Maria's torn dress and dishevelled hair was more than enough to understand what had happened. The three women simply hugged Maria and quietly shared tears together with her. The reality was that these women were also carrying their own share of tragic stories during the war, which were buried within them and never spoken of.

The shop owner consoled her by taking her to her office in the rear of the shop and helped her through the day. Mama felt so impugned, intimidated, humiliated, degraded and dirty even though she managed to avoid the worst insult to any woman that one could ever imagine.

Three months passed and it was already September again. Mama kept habitually praying to 'Our Lady of Czestochowa' with her rosary, hoping it would bring her family back together again one day. That desire and hope was the greatest wish she ever had for her happiness believing that maybe they both survived somewhere.

***

My mama went on and on telling me everything, that was so deeply hurting her, and crying out her entire heart and soul, with the bitter memories of her past. It took her a good many hours to talk about it as it was emotionally very draining, crushing, disturbing and exhausting for her to remember the entire experience in detail. In the heavy moments it was like a total reliving of the whole war and beyond all over again.

My heartfelt empathy for her lamenting sorrows, as well as for my dear brother, made me so very sad that I shed tears with her many times. I was left grieving for both my brother and mama for what they suffered. War is responsible for so many tragedies that it beggars belief how people can survive such hardships. Walter and mama were indeed 'Victims of War.' I tried to console mama as best as I possibly could.

When she told me about her last encounter on the train with the Russian soldier, I was the one shattered in disbelief after listening to what my mother revealed to me. It was a very private memory, which I am certain she undoubtedly intended it to be kept silently buried forever. I sincerely regretted that I kept asking her to tell me that part of her story.

I wished I had never put her through such a deep rooted humiliation of remembering a very private and personal violation committed against her.

With my deepest respect I have only the greatest admiration for my mother, who was a woman of great courage and decency to be able to recall what she experienced and wanted to forget. My mother managed to find the strength to entrust me with her very personal story, for which today I am so grateful to her that she was able to tell me. She was exhausted reliving the experience again after 47 years in silence since 1945. In my heart, I believe that she earnestly intended to take that secret with her to the grave.

The sun was rising. I ordered some breakfast for her, so that she could eat and go to bed for a good rest. After listening to mama's heart wrenching ordeal, which she imparted in such detail, I was also emotionally worn out. The next day we drove home through the timeless Australian desert for three days, mostly in silence. The desert was somehow soothing and the monotony of an empty nothingness meditated our hearts and minds, as we were drifting through red desert sands.

The road was totally straight, stretching to the endless and eternal horizon of a huge all-consuming blue and cloudless sky. When looking from a distance, the vastness of Australia in the "never-never," as the Australian's refer to it appeared to swallow us up into the emptiness and disappear. The awe of the desert left us voiceless and in amazement about our insignificance. Even music in the car disturbed the silence of the soul. After that long journey back to Canberra, it was good to be at home again and reminisce what the desert was able to teach you.

CHAPTER FOUR

Escape to Freedom

The Escape: From Poland & Czechoslovakia

When Germany capitulated the Allies commandeered many estates for their various military Head Quarters and Osterbrock in Germany was one of them. When my father was finally stationed with the British military in Osterbrock, from 9th May 1945 to April 1947, with the Polish First Panzer Division as 2nd Lieutenant, his name may have remained as Michorowski for a while. He requested a leave of absence to return to Poland in late 1945, which was already under the occupied oppression of the Communist Soviet Union, to search for my mother. 'Indefinite leave' was granted to him as Michorowski and he left for Poland dressed in civilian clothes.

My suspicion is that my father might have been a spy for the British MI5, being allowed 'indefinite leave' to travel to Poland, which was already under the Soviet sphere of the 'Cold War', became questionable for me. (I do not believe that the armed forces would give 'indefinite leave' unless there is a specific reason for a service to the country). Regrettably that part of his life remains totally unknown to me. My parents never told me anything about it. However, taking into account that my father lived in the UK for eight months, he would have learnt a great deal of the English language, before he was sent to France for the Battle of Normandy. After all he was a British Officer by then.

My father had with him a lot of gold coins, which he had somehow managed to accumulate during the war that in today's value would be enough to open many doors. I do not know how he carried it with him or how he mysteriously managed to acquire that much gold, as he never told me that enigma either. I can only guess that perhaps he might have had it all sewn into his clothes. I asked my mother one day, long after my father passed away, "How did my father get all that gold?" She simply said that he was able to organize it during the war and never elaborated any further. To this day I have no idea.

In very late 1945 my father was about to enter the new Poland, which was taken over by Soviet Russia and under the restructure of a different ideology in the name of Stalin's communism, which was just another reign of fear. Thankfully he had all that gold with him to be able to bribe guards on trains and at border controls.

Mama was resigned to her fate and the new political environment, as did the rest of Poland. She lived out her life existing in that room all alone, with the bare minimum of possessions as to not upset the communist party officials. Life had to continue after the war and mama was strong enough by then to keep going on living in the hope of seeing her husband again.

It was already very cold and in the dim light of a bleak winter's day, with the snow lightly falling, making way for yet another year to soon pass. My father patiently plodded on to Poland by train. He eventually arrived at the border to find what was left of Poland, which lay in ruins as he made his way to Podlesie, in the hope of finding mama alive and at her old address. He went to her flat and knocked on the door but there was silence.

He anxiously inquired with neighbours as to Maria's whereabouts, hoping not to hear that she was dead. To his relief he was told that she was still working at the same hat shop in Gliwice.

He immediately went there in joyful anticipation and found my mother working in the hat shop. He was dressed in civilian clothes and looked at my mother through the shop window. He was staring at her in bewilderment, silent in mind, frozen in thought just staring at her, as if time stood still, gently waving his hand with a big smile in recognition of her being alive.

He was mesmerized when she recognised him and could see the huge smile light up her face in disbelief to see her Franus. All she could think was that he kept his promise to come back and was alive. Her joy and gratitude was overpowering.

His heart was pounding with immense happiness and relief that she survived, which was beyond words. When mama saw him in the window she was taken aback with disbelief on seeing her beloved Franus. It seemed like a miracle for her that all her prayers were answered. She dropped whatever she was doing and stared at him, keeping that big smile and screamed out.

"Franus! My god it's Franus. It's my husband. I don't believe it. Franus, Franus!"

MARIA FARON
This was how my mother looked when my father found her in Poland **1945**

My father went into the shop and Maria wrapped her arms around him with a joy beyond expression. They both ascended into heaven for a while in the realization that they both survived the war.

Mama was overwhelmed in amazement, as they looked into each other's eyes, their arms around each other overjoyed in happiness and tears. One can only imagine how long the hugging and kissing would have lasted. Looking deep in to each other's souls, mama's mind went into overdrive at lightning speed. Whatever was left of her paralysed heart and soul, she wanted to tell Franus what she had endured for the last two years. Her thoughts exploded, trapped in a spinning whirlwind of everything she wanted to say, but was unable to do so.

"Is this real? Am I dreaming? He survived, he's alive. How can I tell him what happened to our son? I'm going out of my mind, I'm not widowed. Oh god, am I just dreaming? Please god, don't let me wake up. I want it to be real. How can I tell him how I feel? It's impossible!"

Mama's thoughts kept spinning, drowning in her tears from all the pain and sorrow in her heart, almost feeling faint.

"My darling, oh my love, you're alive, you're alive, I can't believe it". She said in blissful joy.

"I promised you that I would come back, didn't I? Oh my god! I'm so happy to find you, thank God you're alive!" Franus replied.

Mama hugged my father tightly, trembling in his arms, not knowing how to tell him that Walter was lost. She looked forlorn, bursting into uncontrollable tears with her intense despair of losing Walter.

"My poor baby, Walter." She said with a broken heart, trying to catch her breath.

She felt limp and fell into a chair. My father instinctively sensed that something had happened to his son. The shop owner took my father aside and told him what happened to Walter, as my mother was sobbing and unable to speak. He held her in his arms and lovingly assured her that they will find him.

"Nobody said that he was dead so we'll find him together, I promise. He's alive somewhere I'm sure. Maria let's go home."

He was deeply distraught and saddened that his son was missing. They could not allow themselves to even contemplate that he might have perished somewhere in the ashes of the war. Such grief was too heartbreaking to even enter their minds.

With tears of joy and sadness they went home.

"Maria darling, you look so much better than when I saw you last. I'm so happy that your TB is under control." Franus said."

As my father entered their flat he was glad to be home with his wife at last. He was taken aback at what he saw, astonished to find the room so drab and sparsely furnished, with only the bare minimum to live out ones' life, in the very modest space she had. He was stunned on seeing what was left of my mama's one-room flat in Podlesie.

Maria told him that the few things she had left after the Germans retreated, the Soviet invasion took place. The madness of communism swept across Poland like a giant tsunami. The new era was like a cleansing of the Bourgeoisie with a new ideology, which was being systematically deployed by Russian soldiers. All citizens were treated with the same contemptuous actions.

Two Russian soldiers forced their way into mama's flat, looked around her flat with scrutiny at her elegant furnishings and anything that was beautiful was 'Bourgeoisie' and her cherished Persian carpet was cut into pieces. All the crystal vases, glasses and the beautiful porcelain crockery and figurines, that she kept from her mother's home, was smashed in defiance of anything reminiscent of the Tsar or any class that opposed the proletariat.

Mama was helpless to stop them and just watched all her things being destroyed in front of her. She begged, implored and beseeched them not to destroy her most loved family treasures and heirlooms, but was unable to change their minds. 'Bourgeoisie' they shouted at her. Mama was left standing in bewilderment and trembling afraid they will trash her entire flat, as they finally marched out speaking in Russian staring at her, and again shouting 'Bourgeoisie' at her. My father just listened in disgust at what she told him.

The downtrodden people of Poland found themselves living under a very different ideology from the Nazis. One wonders which was worse; the Nazis or the Soviets? My father just shook his head at what the new tyranny of communism meant for Poland.

He told mama that he was now a British Officer with the same rank of 2nd Lieutenant. She was amazed and surprised that she became the wife of a British officer this time. Mama had no words left to even think about it. She found it bizarre at the time.

He then decided to get out of Poland as quickly as possible and go west back to West Germany. However, mama was still obsessed with finding her son and she never lost hope of finding him. My mother desperately wanted to go to Prague to find their lost son. Mama still believed in her heart that Walter might be somewhere in Czechoslovakia or taken to Prague by Marta, when she was unconscious in the hospital. So my father agreed and they went to West Germany via Czechoslovakia in search of Walter. My parents were so very much in love and it was that love and trust that saw them through the next hurdles they faced to get out of Poland

They lived for a short time in Podlesie, as if in a kind of limbo, suspended in a dreamlike timeless existence knowing it would soon have to end. They were preparing how to enter Czechoslovakia under communist surveillance, which was difficult when you had to report every move you made.

Christmas and New Year passed by without any celebrations. With the advent of 1946 it was bitterly cold and they left Podlesie in the snow, destined for the town of Cieszyn, which is a small and very old medieval town on the Polish border with Czechoslovakia dating from the 7th century. All they took with them was their documents and a few personal things in two suitcases, knowing that they would never return to Poland again.

The river Olza is the border, which is crossed over by a large covered bridge. My parents made their way to get across that bridge. However, it was not that easy without the correct documents to cross that border. So my father went to see the town Mayor, who was very helpful, for a price of course. He bribed him with some gold to issue false papers for both of them to cross over the bridge; but there was a catch. In the adjoining office there was another person listening in, who was from the Soviet NKVD, *(Narodnyy Komissariat Vnutrennikh Del);* 'The People's Commissariat for Internal Affairs;' Known as the KGB today.

He was with the secret police and entered the office having overheard the conversation.

He was a robust heavily built Russian man with deep blue eyes and black hair, speaking Polish with a thick Russian accent. He approached my father with an intimidating arrogance and a forceful confidence, pressuring him into signing papers to work as a "spy" for the Soviets in the west, or be denied an exit document to cross the border. My father knew that he would never be allowed to leave Poland if he refused to sign the papers.

He had no way out of this predicament except to agree with the secret police agent and accept the proposal, which was really a command by the NKVD and a duty to mother Russia. He felt as if this situation was a repeat of when he was conscripted into the German army in July 1942. But this time his beloved wife, Maria was going with him and would no doubt get mixed up with the spy game and become as expendable as my father.

They both knew what this meant and could do nothing to avoid it. Yet again the irony of being left without a choice, he just looked at the Russian agent without any emotion and picked up the pen to sign.

With total composure my father signed the papers and took his documents. Before he left that office he was told to make sure he would report to the NKVD on arrival and speak to a specific person in Prague, who would advise him about his next assignment. Suddenly my father found himself trapped again, but this time he was forced into working under the Russian flag and agrees to play a new spy game for mother Russia.

This new and unexpected situation thrust upon him became too much to endure, but he had no choice under the circumstances. They both left the office with knotted stomachs, whereupon they proceeded to the bridge and crossed the river Olza fleeing to Prague. He managed to keep calm and controlled to get out of the country.

On arrival in Prague it was a great surprise for them to find that the city was intact and not destroyed by Hitler, unlike Warsaw in Poland. The Czechs did not oppose the forces of Nazi Germany, thus saving their entire mediaeval city, which is exceptionally beautiful, dating from the 9th century. Prague is a magnificent showcase of a master built city with architecture from the medieval period and truly amazing in its preservation.

Of course my father had no intention to comply with orders to spy and avoided being caught by the NKVD. They were living on the run and incognito all the time. In his mind he refused to play the spy game. All he wanted was to find his son and get out of the eastern block and safely return to West Germany with mama.

They kept evading the Russian secret police that were onto their whereabouts, even though they kept on the move. They secretly lived in a small flat in Prague for a while until a man from the Russian intelligence knocked on the door.

My parents were prepared and intuitively knew it was the NKVD and at lightning speed, without a word and in total silence, my mother instantly buried my father under a massively thick and large feather duvet on the bed and made the duvet completely flat.

They were very well rehearsed for such an eventuality. The duvets in that part of Europe are very thick as the winters are fiercely cold. He lay under that duvet without moving and trying to breathe as gently and unnoticeably as possible. The knocking on the door was getting impatient; she moved swiftly and opened the door. It was a man from the NKVD Politburo and speaking in Czech, in which my parents were well versed with by then. He marched into the room.

"Where is your husband?" He asked.

"I'm alone and I don't have any idea where my husband is." She replied, totally hiding her fear. He pulled out his gun, held it in front of her face and angrily asked again.

"Where is your husband?" He sternly glared at her.

My father heard everything and remained still, quiet and terrified that Maria might be shot. He waited, praying that she will manage the situation.

She looked directly into his eyes and then at his gun, trying to keep her calm composure, but was sick in the gut with fear. She started to perspire on her head and the sweat slowly trickled from under her hair and began dripping done the back of her neck, with beads of sweat appearing on her brow and again she answered.

"I told you, I have no idea where my husband is."

After searching the tiny apartment he pressed his gun against her forehead and said.

"You better tell him to report to me immediately when he gets home."

Handing her a piece of paper he said:

"Here are the directions. Do you understand? Make sure he gets it." He then angrily left.

My parents had nerves of steel to be able to endure such a close shave. If my father were caught he would have been either arrested or shot. The next day they left very cautiously in the night bound for the German border. They were so nervous, stressed and frightened with fear of being followed and had to be constantly vigilant with eyes in the back of their heads. They were pensively up-tight, on the lookout to avoid being confronted with the NKVD. After living in Prague for six months and searching every orphanage, they had no choice left, but to abandon their search, 'never finding Walter' in spite of all their efforts. I will never know why they spent six months in Prague to find my brother. They never told me why they spent so much time there, which remains a mystery to me.

They were in a hurry to cautiously leave their flat going straight to the main train station in Prague. They were constantly looking in every direction to make sure they were not being followed. Once at the station they quickly bought a ticket and boarded a steam train bound for the German border.

As the sound of the steam engine roared and pulled away, there was a sigh of relief to get out of Prague and away from the secret police. The moment of departure from the station, they were wracked with intensely stressed emotions and breathless pounding hearts, which was so tense that hey both almost wanted to vomit from fear. They were both terrified of the circumstances they would have had to face if being caught leaving Prague.

Arriving at the West German border they again had to bribe the border guards with gold at the border town of Cheb/Eger, dating from the 12th Century, on the border between West Germany and Czechoslovakia. Unknown to my parents, the border guards were already notified by the NKVD of the possibility that my parents could be coming there.

Inevitably my parents were arrested and interrogated. My father tried to bribe them with gold, but it did not work. My mother was trembling and afraid of what might happen to them, but the guards asked for more gold. The Czech border guards stripped my parents of all their attire and searched through their belongings and clothes.

Finally they found and took the entire gold my father possessed and then debated whether to let them through to the West German side or not. It was a situation of believing either that the border guards would let them go freely or that they would simply shoot them both in the back, as they attempted to cross over into West Germany. The guards loaded their riffles and told them to march and cross over to the West. Franus and Maria believed that this was the end and that they will be shot in the back. My mother knew she was already pregnant with her second child and that made it worse.

As my parents were crossing the border they felt sick, shaking from the trauma, not from losing all their gold, but that they might be shot. Maria put her hand on to her tummy, as if caressing her unborn baby, thinking that this time she will not lose her baby but will take it with her. They held hands tightly and looked at each other, speaking with their facial expressions. They wanted to say, which came from their hearts and eyes in silence, that they loved each other. They were unable to speak with a blank mind, expecting to hear that rifle shot and wanted to go together to wherever one goes after death.

They kept walking and walking, looking into a foggy soundless mist ahead, aware of every sound hearing each footstep made, until they reached the other side and were finally received by the guards in West Germany. They were wet with perspiration and floating in a kind of void of being alive in disbelief.

Miraculously they were alive and joyously on their way to freedom. They could not believe it. They were in amazement that there was no bullet in the back. They survived! They were numbed with their escape, as well as what might await them in a new life, away from war and oppression. Once they were safely in West Germany they looked at one another and with a sigh my father said.

"Oh Maria darling, we may have lost everything but at least we still have each other, let's thank God for that. We made it!" He smiled.

They held their hands together and walked away from that dark world and into another new one of great hope and freedom.

At least they were alive and safe making their way to Osterbrock, West Germany, and freedom. My father knew that he would never be able to return to Poland again, while the country was under the occupation of the Soviet Union. If he dared to go back to Poland he would face immediate arrest at the border and possible execution without doubt.

A new war began known as "The Cold War." Poland was now ruled by fear and oppression where the walls had ears. It was an existence of trusting nobody and daily survival for the Polish people was harsh, which remained that way for the next 45 years. The outside world was closed to them. Only the well-oiled propaganda machine of the Soviet regime was brainwashing the entire nation. Living under such oppression was soul destroying.

When my parents arrived in Osterbrock my father changed into a British uniform with the rank of 2nd Lieutenant. Mama just looked at him with a smile in bewilderment, finding herself the wife of a British Officer. There was nothing for her to say. It was just surreal.

They never gave up looking for their lost son. Mama could not allow herself to give up the search and was so very anxious to find Walter. She kept living in the hope that he might still be alive somewhere. Her strong belief and constant prayers to find her son was unfailing.

That determination was a state of permanent relentless anxiety wanting so desperately to find Walter. The German government, in conjunction with the Red Cross, set-up a bureau in Munich for finding all the children in Germany, who were stolen or kidnapped during the war. A law was passed that anyone who was holding such children was illegal and would be subject to the crime of kidnapping.

The reality of what The Third Reich had planned for Poland was so horrifying and barbaric, that it almost seems unthinkable such an idea could even have been conceived. Yet this planned unimaginable terror scenario took place, like a science fiction story, which was actually unleashed on Poland in 1939, and is too shocking to even perceive as a possibility.

I began to read about the abduction of children by The Third Reich in WWII after listening to my mother's story. To my disbelief as to what Germany had planned for abducted Polish children left me astonished and horrified. Kidnapping of non-Germanic children by Nazi Germany (Polish: abunek dzieci) was an aberration of respect to life itself. Part of the plan involved taking children from the rest of Europe and moving them to Nazi Germany for the purpose of Germanization, or indoctrination into becoming culturally German. The plans for Poland by Himmler and Hitler were truly terrifying.

The aim of the plan was to destroy and extinguish "Polish" as a race, and leave within Poland a considerable slave population to be used within ten years. Hopefully for Germany, Poles would eventually be removed completely within 15 to 20 years. In other words a total genocide was planned for the Polish nation in the end and all of Poland becoming Germany.

Between 1940 and 1945, according to official Polish estimates, approximately **200,000** Polish children were abducted by the Nazis. **"My brother, Walter was one of them."**

My parents went to Munich to seek out if my brother's name was on the list of 200,000 kidnapped children. Munich was in ruins beyond recognition and walking through all the rubble there was one large building still standing, near the centre of the old part of the city, which was the Red Cross. Anxiously they went into the building to find their son's name. There were so many people there, also in search of their abducted children so my father left all his details and whereabouts in Osterbrock. Time passed by and amazingly my brother's name was miraculously found on the list. It took a while to find where he was located in Germany.

My mother was heavily pregnant with me at the time and I was due in late December. Having read the above historical facts, it is truly a miracle that my brother survived such a monstrous and evil plan devised by Hitler and his henchmen. I can only imagine what was going on in the minds and hearts of my parents living purely on hope, after learning that perhaps their son was a victim of Hitler's plan for Germanization, 'which he was.'

I WAS BORN. West Germany, December 1946. It was a freezing winter's morning with the dim light of a dawning dark grey sky. The snow was thickly falling silently and ankle deep, with a gentle wind blowing down the main street of Osterbrock. It looked like a Christmas card. The village was located near the Dutch border.

My parents temporarily lived there because my father was stationed with the British Allied Forces, together with the First Panzer Division of the Polish Army after the war was over. My mother just gave birth to a boy and named me Andreas, on my German birth certificate and later, Andrzej on my Polish birth certificate, issued by the Polish Army, giving me two citizenships at birth.

I was named after my paternal grandfather, as was the custom in that period. My parents were delighted with jubilation to have another son. My birth gave them great joy and comfort to have another son, giving them some relief from pining for the lost one. But most importantly, a few days later my father received news from the Red Cross that their lost son, Walter, was alive in Germany two years after he was kidnapped.

My parents were bewildered, stunned, relieved and overjoyed beyond belief. My mother knelt down in tears of gratitude to pray and thank Our Lady (Virgin Mary) of Czestochowa for answering her prayers. She was overwhelmed beyond imagination with the news.

My brother was located north of Bavaria. With such wonderful news my father got permission from the Army to go and collect him after the New Year in January 1947. So he went by train to Wurztsburg, north of Bavaria to fetch his son. The people who had him were not in Wurzburg but on a farm outside the city.

He made his way there to collect his lost son at the farm of the Aarden family. I can't imagine what the feelings of my parents would have been like with receiving such news. But most of all, what were the feelings of my father on the train journey to Wurzburg?

When I think of what might have been going on in his mind, I can almost hear his heart beating at the moment of anticipation when meeting his first son, whom he had met only briefly once during his furlough from the German Army in 1943. His mind would have been so preoccupied with so many feelings of the amazing survival of his wife and son.

In his hand he clasped the relic given to him by the Dutch priest he met during the occupation of Holland. That relic was a small bone from a saint encased in a brass circular container with a glass top. On the journey his silent contemplative grief of all that he experienced since September 1939 was coming to a focal point on seeing Walter.

On arrival at the farm he met his son, who was very shy and withdrawn speaking with a whisper, but only in German. He no longer spoke any Polish. He only spoke a very poor peasant type of German (known as Plat Deutsch). My father's heart was totally broken when he met Walter to realize how malnourished he was. He was shocked and appalled to see him so neglected and in his shabby old clothes. He was holding back his tears. He looked into Walter's eyes and held him close to him smiling to comfort Walter and make him feel relaxed enough to trust him. Walter had no recollection of his father.

My father then had to explain to Walter, in German, who he was and that he has come to take him home. He was so deeply saddened at the sight of this frail and totally neglected little boy suffering from scurvy, malnutrition, weak, dirty and forlorn, still wearing the same clothes he was kidnapped in two years earlier. Walter was just looking at this man not knowing where he was going to go next.

I will never know what my father might have said to Frau Aarden; because he never told me, and Walter never mentioned it to me either. However, he dressed Walter in the new clothes that mama prepared, which he had with him, and took him back to Osterbrock to join his family. When he arrived at the small house where I was born, my mother was anxiously waiting for him and she just collapsed to her knees on seeing the dreadful condition Walter was in.

She looked into his expressionless eyes, his drawn pale face and threw her arms around him, crying from the depths of her heart and soul. She was shattered into a million pieces, like a shooting star in the night; the reality that he was alive and at last in her arms was explosively numbing. The desperate struggle to find him was finally over.

Mama was angry, horrified and could not believe the cruelty of these people who never cared for him properly. His neglected health and bruises on his head from being hit by Mr Aarden, if Walter spoke loudly, deeply saddened my parents.

She could hardly speak through her choking throat, bursting chest, tears of relief and the passing of a tortured memory. The agonizing search to find him, with the pain and 'guilt' she had lived through for losing him, was never really resolved in her heart. She was 'wailing and wailing' uncontrollably about her "guilt," as she held him in her arms, gradually calming down. She was in a state of bewilderment that the search was over.

"**Guilt!**" Mama would "wail and wail" again in the distant future, 47 years later, on one starry night, deep in the red desert of central Australia at Uluru. It was there that I held her in my arms and said.

"Cry mama, cry and cry as much as you need to cry. I am here with you and for you. Let the pain go. There is no need for you to suffer anymore. **Mama, it was not your fault!** It all happened a very long time ago."

Her wailing in the desert was not about her war experiences but was all about her "guilt." She remained with that "guilt about losing Walter" for the rest of her life, uttering the name of Walter with her last words, as she slowly drifted away into the ether on her death bed.

Walter was soon to be six years old at the end of January 1947. She bathed him immediately and then introduced him to me, Andreas, only just over three weeks old. I was a little baby in my cot and Walter was staring at me not knowing or realizing at that moment, that I was his little brother. Walter did not speak to our parents very much. He was timid and withdrawn. He called his mother 'misses' *(In German; Die Frau, which really means, The Woman),* and it took him three months to call his parents, mama and Tatus (dad). Later on in my teens he told them that he only remembered a long train journey with a woman but could not remember her name.

Mama told me that Mrs Aarden fed Walter a diet of red cabbage with potatoes and he slept in the barn, sometimes with the three daughters of the Aarden family. He spoke of his experiences on the farm that he had to tend to the geese by the river, and how he fell into the water and a local farmer saved his life. Like dark haunting dreams and shadows in the night were these vague memories that plagued him, but unfortunately that part of his life will never be fully remembered or known, as Walter never spoke of it to me. That remains his story. All I know is what my parents told me.

The time came for us to leave Osterbrock and West Germany, one month earlier than my father thought, on 1st March 1947 and journey to Bremerhaven for the voyage to Scotland. I remember my mother telling me of an incident with Walter on the ship sailing to Scotland. He was lost on the ship and naturally mama went out of her mind.

The captain alerted the crew to find Walter and they eventually did. She was almost going crazy with the fear of losing him again, after so desperately trying to find him for two years.

We arrived in Scotland and were finally on the journey to freedom. Mama revealed to me that she was unable to produce milk to breast feed me, so she had to give me Carnation tinned milk; which she heated with a candle on both the ship and train journey until we reached the refugee camp in south west England.

Their anticipation about how will life turn out for them in England was another stressful hurdle to get through. However, they survived so much hardship and trauma in Poland, Czechoslovakia and Germany, that made this new challenge at least a little easier not having to face a war situation. They went forward and bravely managed to carve out a new life for all of us that ended up happily.

CHAPTER FIVE

A New Beginning

My parents in England with all their possessions in two suitcases March **1947**, Culmeed Camp, Taunton, Somerset – England

Under the British flag:

In March 1947 our family life began in England. After arriving by ship on the shores of Scotland we were temporarily housed in a refugee camp. From there the family was transferred to a train and we journeyed southward, down the entire country, until we ended up in Culmeed Camp, North Taunton, Somerset England. All they possessed was in the two suitcases they brought with them and with that they had to start a new life.

Looking tired, forlorn and lost, my parents faced a daunting future having to try and survive exiled in a foreign land. They were without any money and worst of all, no understanding of a new language, especially for mama. Suddenly communication in English became an obstacle of frustrating ordeals, how to make the English people understand them.

Living in the temporary barracks as DPs was depressing, lonely, sad, anxious and filled with the unknown of how to go forward into a world without knowing the language, as well as recovering from the trauma of what they lived through in the war years.

We lived in that camp for over two years. It was there that my father was finally demobbed from the Army on the 8th July 1949 and was free to go and work. His first priority was to find a place in London for us to settle and then find a job. Our new life really started in 1949 when we moved to Montrell Road, Streatham in London, SW2. My mother drummed my name and address into my mind, which I have never forgotten to this day, in case I got lost.

My parents were grateful to finally be in England and experience "Freedom," which was denied under Hitler's Ideology of The Third Reich in Germany during the war. They wanted to heal from the terrible oppression of totalitarianism, under the ideology of Stalin's regime of Communism in Poland. Under communism freedom of speech, freedom of expression, written or spoken was punishable with either prison in the Gulags of Siberia or death. It is that "Democratic Freedom" in England that my father fought for, even though he ended up having to do it in three uniforms. My parents were indeed very courageous people.

My mother was taking care of two boys as well as a husband, who was also a devastated man from his war experiences. There was no such thing as counselling in those days. Many, many tears were shed during their adjustment in exile. They both needed to heal and it took many years. It was from here that I started to have vague memories of mine from the age of three years. A new and wonderful future was awaiting me for which I am so grateful today.

Traumatized war victims had to simply recover alone and live with it until time healed them. These circumstances are not taken into consideration by those who have never been in a war zone. Experiencing the grief of losing everything plus family members, relatives and friends, which these people had endured, is enough to drive a person insane.

In spite of all that hardship, emotional distress and immense challenges, they somehow pulled through and eventually forged on to start a new life in London from 1949. They grieved for the political situation in Poland, as well as being grateful to be in the safety and freedom of living in England. It was a strange paradoxical conflict of emotions.

I will forever admire their courage, tenacity, loving care, respect, responsibility, strength, decency, integrity and the sheer goodness of my parents in being able to carve out a life for their family in the end. My mother remained loving nature, where she always found peace and solace to sooth away her painful memories of the past.

MY FATHER, THE TRIPLE SOLDIER

His incredible endurance and strength of mind with fortitude and courageous perseverance to confront the unknown was amazing. My father's ability to survive so much was indeed admirable. I can only try to mimic and honour my father for his amazing strength of character, not to allow his loving heart to be damaged beyond repair. He always managed to tell jokes with great humour to ease the pain of his war memories, creating a positive outlook for all his family. I will always remember him that way.

He ended up being a wonderful loving father and husband throughout his life until his death, in spite of his shocking experiences in the war.

MY FATHER'S MEDALS WERE FOUND IN 2013

For whatever reason my father had, it was a well-kept secret from the family, until its discovery by me through my investigations in 2013. The mystery of why they were never claimed by my father in 1947 remains an unknown enigma.

However, almost 70 years passed and I was researching my father's war record and after many months I was contacted by the British Department of Defence-Polish in London. I was utterly dumbfounded when I was informed that my father had three WWII decorations left to him by King George VI of England, unclaimed since 1947. I was beside myself with joy, of not only being given his entire war record, but also the notification of his unclaimed medals.

When I requested for the medals to be sent to me I was most disappointed to be advised that I was not entitled to retrieve them if an older sibling was alive. Only the first born was eligible to collect them if still alive or in succession. Or, I could ask for 'consent' from my eldest brother, Walter, to receive them. "That was by way of British Law."

I then excitedly contacted my brother, Walter, and told him about the wonderful news that I discovered our father's medals. I asked for his consent to allow me to collect them. However, one month later, he contacted me to let me know that he refused to give me the consent and decided to claim the medals for himself. They were sent to my brother instead of me. Walter in turn gave them to his daughter, Monique, as a gift and instructed for the medals to be passed on to his two grandchildren. As a result I never got to see the medals and they remained in the possession of my niece in America. Again time passed and I was going to be visited by Monique and her family, which was an unexpected joy for me, since it was two years since I met her in 2012 in America.

AUSTRALIA - DECEMBER 2014

Like an echoing distant voice I could hear Monique speaking.

"Uncle Andrew, hello, Uncle Andrew are you okay?" Monique asked.

She was looking at me with concern as I appeared ready to cry. I heard her voice, as if waking from deep thoughts about my parents during the war. I looked into her eyes and almost unable to speak, with a sigh I just said.

"Oh Monique! Thank you, thank you so very much from the depth of my heart for all your love and kindness. I don't know what to say. This is so incredible."

In disbelief the parcel Monique gave me contained my father's three WWII medals given to him by the British Monarch, HRH King George VI in 1947. They were so unexpectedly in my hands, as if my father was with me in that moment of both grief and joy. My emotions were mixed and many, looking at my father's medals, missing my parents, after writing about their amazing war experiences in the pages which you have just read.

I was grateful to be together with my niece, her family and my partner. As I held my father's medals in my hands I deeply wondered why he never accepted them in 1947. He never told my mother about the medals either. Why? I had to look into my heart and soul-search for a reason why he dismissed such important war decorations from The King of England.

The only reason I could think of was that my father, being a Polish Officer in the Polish Army to defend his country with patriotism and die for Poland did not happen. He ended up in a German and British uniform, which made him see the futility of such a paradox he lived through. Being a philosophical man, experiencing such unique circumstances, he realized that there were no enemies until he was told who the enemy were.

Therefore accepting the medals was also futile and superfluous. He fought to defend his freedom and mostly to survive for the love of his wife and child. I can only surmise that he actually fought for 'Love' until the bitter end to be with his family. His reward was greater than medals, when he was with his loved ones and happy. That is all he wanted. I did indeed have a remarkable father.

After living in London for twenty years I decided to migrate to Australia in 1967. My brother migrated to the USA shortly after I left England. When I experienced the wonders of Australia I fell in love with it and its people. One year later I sponsored my parents to Australia for a better life down under. The best decision I ever made was to help them to come to the land of sunshine and opportunity, where they found great happiness for the rest of their lives.

In contemplation:

I quietly sat alone in the seclusion of my lounge room at home, deep in thought about all that had transpired in my life. The sun was setting and the beams of light penetrated through the room window, illuminating the dust weightlessly suspended in the air. I noticed the buzz of a fly darting through the mist of dust and settle onto the TV screen. I began to daydream. My mind was drifting into another world of the past, remembering the happy times with my parents, as a young boy in London and later in Australia and all our travels in the world.

Experiencing the joys and sorrows in life; this confronts every family no matter how much they try to do their very best, on their journey of life. Knowing and understanding the heart-breaking sadness, when your parents depart from this world is a reminder that it is forever.

I realized how precious love and life is, only when you have lost it.

All that happened now rests in the ether diffusing into eternity. I felt like I was on a cloud of no return, taken on a fast track journey through time, which I had finally completed. I was so grateful to my darling niece, Monique, for being part of my life. I was drifting through a labyrinth of many memories in between the windmills of my mind; awed by the experiences that one lifetime could endure, as it did for my parents during WWII.

It felt as if my soul was watching no more than an illusion of dreams that were not real and yet tangible and took place. They actually existed and were experienced by my parents. I could no longer comprehend how it was possible to experience so much in a lifetime, daunted with all that I had written about my parents. I felt as if I was concluding my entire journey of life, that the only true reality left for me was 'Love.'

My parents survived the war purely on their deep belief and faith in 'Love' and found each other again in the end. A long time ago my father once told me, with a compassionate and loving heart, and said:

> "Life is an art. Living is an Art.
> One has to learn how to live that art."

He was so right. I wish to follow his example. He was my hero.

With that I woke up from my daydreaming pondering thoughts and landed into the present, wondering where destiny would take me until God, 'The Universe,' calls me elsewhere.

THE TRIPLE SOLDIER And My Mother

RETRIEVED IN 2013

ON HER BRITANNIC MAJESTY'S SERVICE
MY FATHER'S BRITISH MEDALS

FRANCISZEK FARON

Born. 27th September 1913, Silesia, Poland
Died. 26th February 1978 Canberra, Australia
2nd Lieutenant: Allied Armed Forces
Infantry No. 3 Supply Company, 1st Armoured Division, 1st Polish Corps. **World War II. 1939 – 1945. Europe.**

BRITISH WAR RECORD

These are the records sent by the DEPARTMENT OF DEFENCE From the United Kingdom ON HER BRITANNIC MAJESTY'S SERVICE

FRANCISZEK FARON was decorated for services by the British in 1947 for the following:

MINISTRY OF DEFENCE
APC DTSCLOSURES 5 (POLISH)
Building 60, RAF Northolt
West End Road
Ruislip, Middlesex HA4 6NG
Telephone: 020 8833 8603 Fax: 020 8833 8866
E-mail: NOR-Polish DiscofficeAsst@mod.uk

Mr Andrew Faron   Our Ref: 3/P/12155/APC/POL/K
                                   Date: 7 November 2013

Dear Sir,

Thank you for your recent enquiry. I am pleased to confirm the following particulars of the military service of:

P/1255-SECOND LIEUTENANT (INFATRY) FRANCISZEK FARON
Born on: 27 September 1913 at Orzesze, Pszczyna, Slqsk, Poland
Parents: Andrzej and Maria nee Zalqc
Marital Status (while serving): Married to Maria Superniok on 21.03.1941
Nationality: Polish Religion: Roman Catholic
Civilian Occupation (prior to **Army Service**): Court Clerk

Service with the Polish Forces under British Gommand:
From: 29 March 1944 to 12 August 1947
Service with the Polish Resettlement Corps: Enlisted on / Commissioned 13 August 1947
Relegated to: Class "W" Reserve on 26 August 1948 unemployed List

Finally discharged: relinquished commission on 8 July 1949 **(honourably discharged)**

Conduct: His record and service were satisfactory

Former Service and History:
Called up from the Reserve on 30.08.1939, he took part in the 1939 September campaign in Poland 01 .09.1939-18.09.1939. Taken prisoner of war by the Germans, according to his own statement, he escaped on 30.09.1939 and returned home to Mikolow, district of Pszczyna, county of Slqsk, Poland, which after the 1939 September campaign in Poland. Annexed by the German Third Reich. Consequently he was conscripted and served in the German Army from 23.07.1942 to **28.11.1943, when he escaped and was taken prisoner of war by the British Allied Army in ltaly.**

"Theatre of Operations."
France, Belgium, Holland and Germany 29.07.1944 to 08.05.1945
01.08.44 - 06.09.44   Action at Caen, Falaise, Abbeville. FRANCE
06.09.44 – 16.09.44   Ypres, Roulers, Thielt, Ghent, St Nicholas. BELGIUM
16.09.44 – 22.09.44   Koewacht, Axel-Hulst. HOLLAND
28.09.44 – 02.10.44   Merxplas, Baarle-Heide, BELGIUM
03.09.44 – 08.11.44   Baarle-Nassua, Gilze, Breda, Moerdijk. HOLLAND
09.11.44 – 08.04.45   Action on the River Maas. HOLLAND
14.04.45 – 08.05 45   Kusten Canal, Aschendorf, Papenburg, Ihrhove, Leer. GERMANY
09.05.45 – April 1947 Allied Occupation Forces of Germany.

Medal Entitlement:
Polish: Army Medal
British: 1930 – 45 Star, France & Germany, the War Medal 1939 – 1945

He served in the United Kingdom and on the Continent from 1944 to 1947. Due to gradual demobilisation of the Polish Forces under

British command he was commissioned in the Polish resettlement Corps (PRC) and served in the United Kingdom until finally relinquishing his commission on 08.07.1949 on absorption into industry.

Commissioned in the rank of 2nd Lieutenant on 23.10.1944

****

It is interesting to note that the date of my parents' wedding date is incorrect in the British war record. They were married in 1940 and not 1941. Also his enlistment to the Wehrmacht was on 25.07.1942 according to the German record, and not the 23rd. Sometimes records are incorrect when language barriers occurred, creating misunderstandings and mistakes.

I kept investigating my father's war records with the German Department of Defence. After many months I finally managed to find out when and where my father was enlisted into the German Army (Wehrmacht). I was so very grateful to the German Defence Department in Berlin, who contacted me and sent me the letter with the details I asked for.

The German war record, regarding my father's time in the German Army is in the following letter from the German Defence Department in Berlin.

****

THE TRIPLE SOLDIER And My Mother

MY FATHER'S GERMAN RECORD

Deutsche Dienststelle BERLIN

für die Benachrichtigung der nachsten Angehorigen
Von Gefallenen der ehemaligen deutschen Wehrmacht
Datum:19.08.2016

(Herrn Andrew Faron) Dear Mr Andrew Faron,
On your request of the 06.07.2016, sent to us from the Generalkonsulat of the Bundesrepublik Deutschland, Sydney, Australia.
 I share with you that Franz Faron, born on the 27.09.1913 in Orzesze.
 Franz Faron was conscripted into the Wehrmacht in Breslau to the first company of the infantry replacements Battalion 7 on 25.07.1942.
 The personal documents of your father (f.e. Wehrpass, Wehrstammbuch, Sotdbuch), are not recorded in our department. Because of this our information is limited to other primary sources of the former German Wehrmacht, the Waffen-SS or other military / militarized associations from the time of the second world war (among this the recognize-tag-directories and loss of documents) and we do not make a claim that our information is complete. Also in individual cases we also have to get our information of secondary sources like e.g. the available war literature.
 Provisionally I need to explain to you that the period of your request could take up to six months.
 <u>Please also let us know when your father died with us?</u> We have no record of his survival after he was missing in action in northern Italy in November 1943.

Sincerely, On behalf,

Geschdftszeichen:
Geschdftszeichen:
(Bei Ruckfragen bitte Geschaftszeichen,

Namen und Geburtsdaten angeben)
IIBI/ Faron, Franz, 27.09.1913
Bearbeiter/in:
Zimmer: Frau xxxxx
Telefon: 030 41 904-340/ -1 39
Telefax 030 41 904-100

****

Many months passed and I received another document from Berlin with more information about my father's war record. I was amazed to receive that letter and am so very grateful to the German War Office in Berlin. They went to the trouble of making an effort to give me his war record, as best as they could find, in spite of the sparse records that were left from so much information being lost in the war.

Once I received these German War Records I was thrilled to discover the exact same dates in both records, British and German, showing that my father was captured by the British on 28.11.1943. Then reading the German War Records that my father was 'missing in action' on 28.11.1943 at the Battle of Sangro in Italy. The jigsaw puzzle was finally completed.

****

Deutsche Dienststelle BERLIN

für die Benachrichtigung der nachsten Angehorigen
Von Gefallenen der ehemaligen deutschen Wehrmacht

(Herrn Andrew Faron) Dear Mr Andrew Faron,
On your request of the 06.07.2016, sent to us from the Generalkonsulat of the Bundesrepublik Deutschland, Sydney, Australia. We now send you his records.

Datum: 10.12.2016

Franz Faron, born on the 27.09.1913 in Orzesze, Krs. Press O/S
Erkennunsmarke: (Tag number or identity disc) 2034 - I. E. B. 7

Grenadier-Regiment 146; Infantry-Division, Battalion 7

1. Antwerp in Belgium, September / October 1942.
2. Vissingen in Holland, November 1942 to June 1943.
3. Ferrara in Italy, July 1943.
4. La Spezia in Italy, August to September 1943.
5. **Fiume Sangro in Italy, 28.11.943. (Sangrotal / Suditalien vermisst) Missing in Action**

AUTHOR'S NOTES

Writing the story of my parents' survival during WWII has indeed been a truly difficult and heart-wrenching undertaking. Having to remember and emotionally feel what they must have felt from what they told me also made me shed tears along the way. After WWII ended people were so relieved to start living again. Those who were left behind and trapped into a world of dictatorial oppression were sacrificed to a life of psychological and physical hardship. Another endurance of totalitarianism reigned over Eastern Europe until 1990.

I wondered if the world would ever change to be a place of love, freedom and acceptance, as it should be. Would humanity ever rise spiritually above having wars and hateful greedy egoistical controllers that we have endured for millennia, ordering us to die for them? In my mind, there is no such thing as religion or barbaric ideologies and enemies, which have all been invented, seducing our minds into believing in hoaxes and lies to control all of us.

After what my parents lived through in WWII, I wondered naively and asked myself: 'Would I live long enough to see a world at peace?' Since my birth in 1946 I have never seen a world without a war somewhere. I just sat alone in my lounge room at home, numbed in a daze, wondering where humanity is going. When will we ever see the 'abolition' of ignorance, bullets and war machines, poverty, crime, starvation, dirty politics, religious hate caused by divisiveness, insatiable greed, aggression and insane wars?

I know that what I am yearning for is a ridiculous and unrealistic pipe dream of a loving ideology, in a world that we all currently live in. Such hope is a hopeless dream that will never happen. It is only possible for those who choose to change their own lives for themselves. Whatever you think, it is a wonderful dream to wish for; even if it is impossible.

The reality of what is again happening in the world in 2016, and after writing my parents' war story of WWII was frightening enough to comprehend. I ask; where are we now?

Look at our world today in 2016. Since 9/11 in 2001, the war in North Africa is raging and continuing to destroy the Middle East, creating millions of refugees yet again, affecting many nations globally. The aggression is spreading like a cancer to other countries in Africa and beyond. Why is this happening? War tragedies, atrocities and barbaric killings continue to augment. I really don't understand why we allow for this to happen. It is an outrageous insult to our human intelligence and consciousness.

We owe it to ourselves to put an end to this shocking insanity. We are all tired of wars!

We watch TV daily as millions are maimed, made homeless, orphaned, lost, traumatized and killed! Humanity is currently witnessing the highest levels of displaced people on record in 2016, since WWII. An unprecedented 65.3 million people around the world have been forced from their homes. What kind of a future world will our young inherit, if we do not do anything to change our minds to rid ourselves of wars? It is time we look deeply into our hearts and ask ourselves: Do we want war?

'Not changing one's mind only leads to prolonged ignorance.'

When I think of what my parents endured during WWII, and how it affected so many millions of people, leaves me speechless. I wonder how our world would look today if all that energy, so insanely consumed, was actually spent on improving everyone's lives instead of destroying it. Imagine it for just a brief moment.

We must hope that 'Love & Peace' will capture our hearts and minds one day. Let war become remembered as a demonic primitive and medieval practise in our global history; from which we have progressed enough to be abhorred to repeat any further wars in the future. Only then 'WAR itself' can become a crime against humanity, illegal and stopped.

ACKNOWLEDGEMNT

I wish to acknowledge my dearest partner, Jeong Wook Jang, to whom I am sincerely indebted. He tirelessly helped me with the editing and structuring of my story through the most difficult parts, which were deeply emotional for me.

Thank you for your patience and love for standing by me when I needed you.

ABOUT THE AUTHOR

Escaping Stalinist Poland, Andrew's parents lived in Germany for one year, where Andrew was born in 1946. The family went to England in 1947 as refugees. Andrew grew up in London, where he learnt to speak English from five years of age. Being stateless he became a British citizen with his family in 1959. His formative years from 1947 to 1967 were difficult, with a dual language and cultural upbringing, which was stressful trying to understand where he fitted in. As the years passed by into adulthood Andrew received a rich education, which gave him greater opportunities. He migrated to Australia in 1967 at 20 years of age. Soon after, he sponsored his parents to Australia for a better life. From there his life changed dramatically when Andrew joined Qantas Airways Ltd., as cabin crew in 1971 and resigned in 2002. The greatest education he ever imagined came about from his worldly travels beyond expectations. Andrew is bilingual, English / Polish and has a reasonable understanding of Czech, Ukrainian and basic German. After retiring he lived in Malaysia and New Zealand for several years before returning home to Australia. He is grateful to be here to tell his parents' story, which would have been an emotionally challenging and difficult undertaking to attempt.